San Francisco
Museum of
MODERN
ART
50 YEARS

This book is published on the occasion
of the exhibition **Robert Hudson:
A Survey** organized by the San Francisco
Museum of Modern Art and supported
by a grant from the National
Endowment for the Arts and a
generous gift in memory of Mason Wells.
The San Francisco Museum of Modern
Art is supported in part by the California
Arts Council, the Institute of Museum
Services, the National Endowment for
the Arts, the San Francisco Foundation,
and the San Francisco Hotel Tax Fund.

Designer: Suzanne Anderson-Carey
Composition: petrographics/typeworld
Printing: GraphiCenter

Front cover: 28. *Running through the
Woods*, 1975
Back cover: Robert Hudson with
Outrigger, 1984 photo: Harvey Stein

Photography credits:
Photographs of the works of art have
been supplied, in many cases, by the
owners or custodians of the works, as
cited in the Checklist of the Exhibition.
The following list applies to photographs
for which an additional acknowledge-
ment is due.
Ben Blackwell: cat. 28
Robert Buchanan: cats. 70, 71, 89
eeva-inkeri, Courtesy Allan Frumkin
Gallery: cats. 68, 94, 98
M. Lee Fatherree: cats. 3, 9, 15, 18, 25, 34,
36, 40, 44, 50, 52, 55, 56, 62, 69, 77, 92,
103, 105, 107, 108, 110, 114
Courtesy Fuller Goldeen Gallery: cats. 13, 54,
88, 91
Greg Heins: cats. 60, 63, 87
Daniel T. Magidson: cat. 59
Adam Reich, Courtesy Allan Frumkin Gallery:
cat. 58
Malcom Varon: cat. 106
Richard Wuertz: cat. 112

Library of Congress Cataloging in Publication Data

Hudson, Robert, 1938-
    Robert Hudson, a survey.

    Bibliography: p. 77.
    1. Hudson, Robert, 1938-   —Exhibitions.
I. Beal, Graham William John, 1947-   II. Butterfield, Jan, 1937-
III. Schwager, Michael, 1953-   IV. San Francisco
Museum of Modern Art. V. Title.
N6537.H74A4 1985   709'.2'4   85-8239
ISBN 0-918471-02-8

Robert Hudson A SURVEY

San Francisco Museum of Modern Art

Foreword *by David S. Rubin*

Essays *by Graham W. J. Beal,*
Jan Butterfield,
and Michael Schwager

Schedule of the Exhibition:

San Francisco Museum of Modern Art
27 June – 18 August 1985

Albright-Knox Art Gallery, Buffalo
15 November 1985 – 5 January 1986

The Art Museum at Florida International
University, Miami
9 May – 6 June 1986

Laguna Beach Museum of Art, California
7 August – 5 October 1986

Contents

Robert Hudson is somewhat of a magician. The magic that he performs is in his ability to juggle seemingly incongruous forms and mediums, and bring them all into balance with remarkable ease. From the painting of complex sculptures in the sixties through combining painting and found objects in the eighties, Hudson demonstrates an adventurous spirit as he continues to challenge barriers that have traditionally existed between mediums. For this reason, *Robert Hudson: A Survey* includes sculpture, painting, drawing, ceramics, and constructions. In addition, there is a playful spirit in Hudson's work that appears frequently in the form of visual puns. Interacting with Hudson's art should provide viewers with many moments of delight.

It has been a pleasure working on this exhibition as its guest curator. I wish to thank the many individuals whose efforts have contributed to the success of the exhibition.

First, I wish to thank Henry T. Hopkins, Director of the San Francisco Museum of Modern Art, for inviting me to work on this project, which has given me the opportunity to deepen my understanding of Bay Area art of recent years. Michael Schwager, Curatorial Assistant, has once again proven that he is an invaluable asset to the Museum. Michael's sincere and hardworking approach to coordinating all aspects of the exhibition is greatly appreciated. I also wish to thank Graham Beal, Michael Schwager, and art critic Jan Butterfield for their perceptive essays on the art of Robert Hudson.

Many other members of the Museum's staff have provided integral expertise and assistance in the organization of the exhibition. Anne Munroe, Exhibitions and Publications Coordinator, has been involved in the orchestration of the exhibition from its inception and oversaw the editing and production of the catalog. Tina Garfinkel, Associate Registrar/Exhibitions, has organized the transportation of artwork, and Julius Wasserstein, Gallery Superintendent, has worked with the very talented members of his installation crew to implement a most complicated installation. The bibliography for the catalog was compiled by Eugenie Candau, Librarian, and additional catalog research was done by Junko Iwabuchi, Museum Intern. Suzanne Anderson-Carey, Graphic Designer, has worked with the design department to create this handsome catalog. Robert Whyte, Director of Education, Beau Takahara, Education Department Coordinator, and Miriam Grunfeld, Assistant Director of Education, have organized an excellent symposium to encourage public dialogue about the art of Robert Hudson.

In planning an exhibition of this scope, we depend upon an artist's gallery representatives for providing information about the location and availability of works. For their generous time and cooperation, I am grateful to Diana Fuller, Dorothy Goldeen, and Chantal Guillemin of the Fuller Goldeen Gallery, San Francisco, and to Allan Frumkin and George Adams of the Allan Frumkin Gallery, New York.

In order to present a full picture of an artist's work over several years, we must ask the cooperation of private individuals and public institutions who are in possession of the work. To the lenders to the exhibition, thank you for your willingness to allow works from your collection to be presented to the public. Special thanks to Byron Meyer for sharing with me your personal insights about the works in your collection.

Finally, it has been a rewarding experience working with Robert Hudson and his wife, Mavis Jukes, on the development and implementation of the exhibition. Curation of the exhibition was a collaborative effort, and I wish to thank Bob and Mavis for their thoughts and suggestions and for the time and patience that each devoted in the process. It is in the spirit of togetherness that we celebrate the art of Robert Hudson.

David S. Rubin
Director of Exhibitions
San Francisco Art Institute

Welded Irony: The Sculpture of Robert Hudson

by Graham W. J. Beal

Robert Hudson's sculptures are a virtual assault on the senses: spacially and formally complex, they contain moveable elements as well as found objects and are, moreover, painted in a wide variety of brilliant colors. With the exception of a relatively austere period around 1970, Hudson has always worked this way, and even his earliest exhibited sculpture, made when he was still in art school, consisted of ingeniously composed and brightly painted metal components. Saying he "loves to take on too much... to be in a position of being overwhelmed," Hudson has consistently refused to limit his approach to sculpture to one aspect at a time.[1] Because of this, it is not easy to trace the kind of development usually discernible in other artists' work, in which issues such as color, form, and scale tend to be addressed one by one and are gradually brought together in a unified whole. Instead, what can be seen in Hudson's career is an approach, if not actually a given style, established very early on—precociously even—followed by a long, almost continuous, refinement and enlargement of the issues stated at the onset. Changes within Hudson's sculpture have tended to be of degree rather than of kind, and though, at different times, various elements of Hudson's sculpture gain importance at the expense of the others, the overall balance remains the same, as does the inimitably exuberant effect of his inclusive style.

Growing up in Richland, Washington, Hudson went to school with William T. Wiley and William Allan (an extraordinary confluence of talent in such an artistically out-of-the-way place). Here their main source of "high art" was art magazines through which they followed developments in remote New York. An equally vital influence was that of their high school art teacher, Jim McGrath, who stressed the openmindedness toward materials and sources that has been such a striking feature of his erstwhile pupils' art. McGrath, who has strong links with the Native Americans of that area, also took Hudson and his friends to tribal ceremonies that, in contributing to their notion of what "art" could be, profoundly impressed the adolescent artists.

Arriving at the California School of Fine Arts (now the San Francisco Art Institute) in 1957, Hudson found the place positively teeming with conflicting ideas and attitudes. On one hand were teachers like Frank Lobdell and Elmer Bischoff: mature talents of the painterly abstract and figurative traditions, who held clear and deeply felt ideas of what art should be about. Lobdell's attitude, for example, was characterized by Peter Plagens in his lively account of California art, *Sunshine Muse,* as painting "as if compositional choices were ethical imperatives." Against this was the work of a younger group of artists (some of whom were based in Los Angeles), such as Edward Kienholz and Bruce Connor, through whose vision the detritus of the urban world was transformed into assemblage sculpture that managed to be both compelling and somehow repellent. Jeremy Anderson's carved sculptures with their connotations of folk art and surrealism offered yet another

vision. Finally there was, in Hudson's mind the most important single group, the students themselves including Joan Brown, Ronald Davis, William Geis, Cornelia Schulz, and Carlos Villa, as well as his old friend, Wiley. The energy level, he recalls, was astonishing: "People were doing every kind of thing; a thousand open doors and you could walk through any one. It was great."

One of the doors that Hudson "walked through" at this time led to theater. Intrigued by a San Francisco Mime Troupe performance at the San Francisco Art Institute in 1960, Hudson proposed a collaboration. Hudson eventually involved Wiley and Wally Hedrick "who," Hudson says, "was knowledgeable about sound and wiring." An elaborate event evolved: "We wired up the theater, a small San Francisco theater, and we did a week and a half's worth of performance. No artists saw it, but we filled the place up every night. All the seats were wired to speakers underneath so that everybody could hear part of what people were saying. Action came off the stage into the audience. It was choreographed, but only loosely, and I loved that." As in his sculpture, for the theater Hudson proceeded on all fronts at once, and this one-time commitment on Hudson's part extended to an involvement lasting for over a year.

In this rich mixture of talent and ideas, the Bay Area art scene paralleled that of New York where a similar transition from late Abstract Expressionist painting to formats more receptive to non-art imagery and materials was going on. Hudson quickly turned away from a full-blown "assemblage" technique in all its cobwebby manifestations, and began to experiment with forms of polychrome sculpture. In taking this course Hudson was accompanied by Manuel Neri and Geis, but, whereas the work of Neri and Geis evolved toward the figurative, Hudson's remained, and has continued to be, essentially abstract. Though his sculpture is frequently anthropomorphic, the unequivocal figure is a rarity in his work, and the first explicit appearance of one—a matchstick man at that—did not occur until the giant 1982 work, *Hot Water* (p. 16).

The basic components of Hudson's sculpture are complex geometric shapes made of welded steel which are then painted. The most notable exceptions to this rule are the extraordinary ceramics created in a two-year collaboration with Richard Shaw, but, in Hudson's ceramics, the figurative elements that appear in each piece of sculpture are subsumed into a quite unfigurative whole. To read Hudson's work as a disguised or tongue-in-cheek form of figuration is to distort the artist's intentions. Figurative elements abound, to be sure, but they are subordinate features at the service of larger perceptual concerns.

Looking at the work Hudson produced in the five years between 1963 and 1968, it is tempting to conclude

---

1. Unless otherwise noted, all quotations are taken from conversations with Robert Hudson and the author in January 1985.

that he tried just about every sculptural and pictorial trick in the book. In keeping with his own desire to take on everything at once, he created complex and audacious works that both exhilarate and tantalize the viewer. On one hand each sculpture is a positive—aggressive even—assertion: they are quite sizeable, have a sense of contained energy, and are brightly hued and variegated. On the other hand, they are precarious-looking structures which, penetrated by space, seem to teeter on the verge of collapse. Furthermore, in his use of paint, Hudson balances color values very carefully: assertive reds and yellows are balanced by recessive pale blues and neutral tans; most importantly, he persistently uses painted geometric forms to contradict the actual geometry of the metal components.

Hudson has consistently explored questions of form and illusion. On occasion his sculptures deal directly with metamorphosis: in *Ear to Year,* 1983-84 (cat. 48), for example, a weird, lopsided face appears and dissolves as it is walked around. In such a case, Hudson's work is clearly linked to that of his longtime friend Wiley. Chance, too, plays a role in the evolution of a Hudson piece, but it is a subordinate role, and, in the end, there is little psychologically or emotionally open-ended about a Hudson sculpture. Surprise, even incongruities, abound throughout his work, but decoding an individual piece, sorting out the flat bits from the three-dimensional pieces, is more a matter of solving a puzzle than launching into uncharted realms of the subconscious mind. Tensions in Hudson's work derive mainly from his ability to bring into play and hold in balance an astonishing array of factors. In one sculpture he can juxtapose immaculately found objects and paint them all in such a way as to blend or confuse their identity. The viewers' sense of reality is challenged by Hudson's ability to balance opulence and treachery. That Hudson's work has such features dealing with positive and negative values encourages its interpretation in poetic terms, referring to notions of infinity, duality, or relativity, but Hudson himself remains intrigued with physical phenomena rather than metaphysical questions.

Hudson's earliest work contains distinctly organic forms. In Untitled, 1963 (p. 33), there is no mistaking the bits of male anatomy that pierce through other, marginally more geometric, elements. The sculpture is literally visceral or, to put it more colloquially, "gutsy," and Hudson's admiration for such distinct but related artists as Marcel Duchamp, Joan Miró, and Arshile Gorky could hardly be clearer. Duchamp's paintings of 1912 presented the human being as a plumbing construct, and he was soon to explore the concept of the male as a machine. It was also Duchamp who pioneered the concept of the "found object": the mundane artifact that, simply by the artist's selection,

becomes part of, if not actually, a work of art itself. Miró's paintings, and later his sculpture, aggressively pursued the theme of procreation and were characterized by an energetic yet sensuous line and bold use of color. Gorky's paintings, direct descendants of Miró's, emphasized a more expressive use of color and a gestural brushstroke. But especially significant for Hudson at this time was David Smith, the American sculptor who had almost single-handedly pioneered a new sculptural technique: welding. Though throughout the twentieth century, artists such as Pablo Picasso, Naum Gabo, and Antoine Pevsner created sculpture from "modern" materials—tin, cardboard, Plexiglas—it was left to Smith (who had learned welding techniques in the 1920s and perfected them in a wartime assembly plant) to establish this industrial technique as *the* modern way of fabricating sculpture. In time, of course, it became something of a cliché, but in the early 1960s it was a fresh approach with seemingly infinite possibilities. Smith had, moreover, started his career as a painter and after 1960 used color as an integral part in almost half of his sculptures.

Hudson was, then, looking in two directions: first, at his teachers and peers in California; second, at the work of several of the great figures of twentieth-century art. It is a measure of his precocity that, by his mid-twenties, he had forged a wide range of influences into an authentically individual style rooted in ambiguous form.

These qualities of ambiguity are clearly stated in works dating from as early as 1964. In *Fat Knat* (p. 11), for example, certain elements are distinctly entomological: a red proboscis and winglike flaps on the top of the barrel-shaped body that seems to hover above a thin green stem. The overall effect is quite comic, right down to the fact that the proboscis is bent upwards at the end. But nothing in the sculpture actually resembles a real bug, and Hudson certainly did not set out to make a funny sculpture of a "hot-rod" insect. For his sculpture Hudson works without preparatory drawings or models; the process of making sculpture is, in a sense, one of discovery for him. From materials around him Hudson begins to assemble a work, adding and subtracting as he goes. Often, as was the case with *Fat Knat,* at a certain point the configuration suggests a title in the artist's mind which in turn suggests a final resolution for the sculpture. Apart from its function as a convenient label, the title *Fat Knat* is just one component in the overall sculpture and, Hudson hopes, another point of entry for the viewer. Looked at in one way, the work looks somewhat like a cartoon bug. Looked at from another aspect, *Fat Knat* is a deft exercise in conflicting form, texture, and color that required painstaking craft and considerable discipline. Twenty years later, Hudson still vividly recalls the acute boredom experienced in painting the little black-and-white checkerboard pattern on the crumbled pipe.

Ambiguity often tips over into a sort of contained absurdity in Hudson's work. It is easy to smile in front of one of his improbable creations. Lively, colorful, and impudent, this is a response encouraged by the artist and reinforced by his penchant for witty titles. Puns (as an example of verbal ambiguity) are common: *Cowboy Saddle Light*, 1974 (cat. 26), *Still Works*, 1970 (cat. 20); alliteration, assonance and rhymes abound: *Fat Knat, Dog Leg,* 1983 (cat. 46), *Five in Disguise*, 1976 (cat. 30). But Hudson is also frequently content to leave a work untitled, and let the forms speak for themselves; that they always do so with a friendly smile derives from their inherent liveliness and the ambiguity of Hudson's sculptural vocabulary.

Organic references in Hudson's work had faded by the mid-sixties. Though he concedes that in the 1964 work *Inside Out* (cat. 7) "there might be a feeling of a weird animal in that big pipe with the E shape," he basically embarked on this sculpture as an essay in drawing in space; an attempt to extend the limits of the medium; and, most particularly, a chance to exploit the malleable qualities of soft pipe metal favored by the gold miners that he brought back from the foothills of the Sierras. Taking this metal, he says, "I heat it up with a torch and then I can fold it like soft clay; it wrinkles and folds over like dough, or like honey off a spoon."

The forms of *Inside Out* seem to dance and give the impression of being suspended in the manner of mobile sculpture by Alexander Calder. Hudson has frequently incorporated actual moving parts into his sculpture—already highly agitated in composition and painted surface. As in the case of Calder, he avoids motorized parts, using instead parts so finely machined that they move for a considerable period—as long as forty-five minutes—simply by being pushed. Just about the whole of *T Table* (cat. 10), also from 1964, spins on its base creating a giddy merry-go-round with forms that, even when actually at rest, appear to tumble across the table.

Many of the upper elements in *T Table* are painted in hard lacquer colors, a measure of Hudson's response to the hot-rod or car culture phenomenon for which California, Southern California especially, is renowned. Hudson was fascinated by the way that bright candy-apple red, brilliant blues, and sheeny silver colors reflected off each other and the things around them (he was to explore this aspect of illusory space in a more focused fashion several years later), and, at the time he made *T Table,* he was exploiting the lacquer colors to add yet another confusing dimension to an already gloriously complicated situation. As a finishing touch (and a neat allusion to car culture), Hudson capped each end of the jointed silver pipe with convex rear-view mirrors through which a wide-angled and therefore distorted version of the spectator's space is sucked into the hectic microcosm of the sculpture's space.

A work of almost baroque daring, and a classic of this early period, is the 1966 *Space Window* (p. 36). At the time he made *Space Window,* Hudson was mindful of the

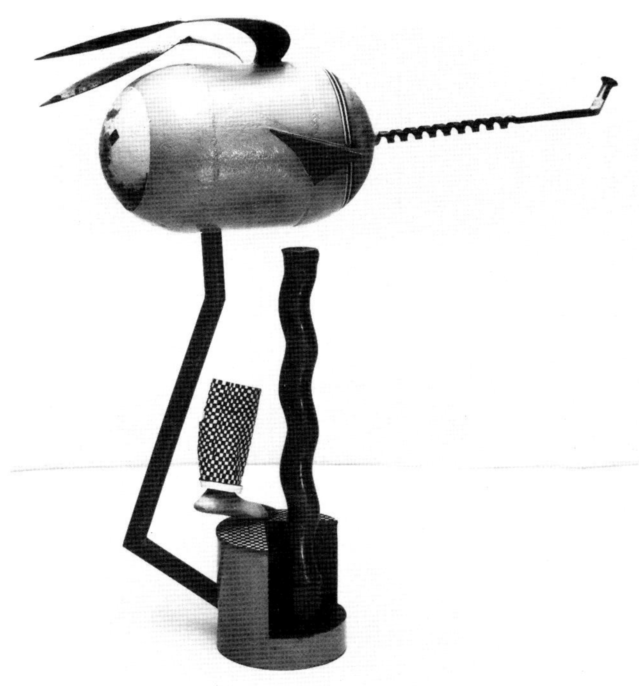

NASA activity that was so prominent a feature of the daily news as America prepared to land a man on the moon. Los Angeles artists were actually availing themselves of "space age" technology for their works, but Hudson's gloss on such activities was very different. Taking the NASA logistical term "space windows," Hudson incorporated painted and sculpted windows into the work, pursuing his interest in real and illusory space. The strangely shaped components that constitute this visual cacophony defy easy description: twisted elipses, cylinders half-flattened at one end, and thick spiraling pipes are intermingled with cubes, triangles, and other more familiar geometric shapes. To complicate matters further, many of the forms are painted in a trompe l'oeil, cloudy sky effectively dematerializing them while other flat elements are given bogus volume by having perspectival views of cubes painted on them. In composition the whole sculpture seems to be in a state of frantic activity, as if subject to powerful centrifugal forces. The sense of variety and of movement is as great as in any Hudson sculpture before or since, but the work is far from kinetic. The only movable features are, in fact, the mundane castors that, in a sense, mock the supersonic pretensions going on above.

In every aspect of this quintessential work, Hudson gives as much as he takes away: form and void, illusion and fact are inextricably intermingled. But this is no excursion into West Coast Zen. Rather it is thoroughgoing irony in the modernist tradition, and it is irony, defined as feigned ignorance designed to confound or provoke, that lies at the very heart of Hudson's work, embracing not only his gently chiding titles but also his bewilderingly inclusive approach to form. *Space Window,* though amusing at one level, is not simply a Rube Goldberg joke at the expense of technology and technologically obsessed artists: it is an investigation of form and how we perceive it. That Hudson does not mind undercutting his own investigation with painted decals and furniture wheels is a logical part of the process. The overt statement conveys the opposite of what is really intended: his work presents a facade of good-natured banter, but behind the facade lies a series of perceptual concerns. The mid-sixties in Northern California were the heyday of "Funk" art; its practitioners—mainly sculptors and ceramicists—were noted for their raucous formal vocabulary and their raunchy subject matter. It is, in a way, just another irony to add to Hudson's persistent use of it that he should have been so widely regarded as the epitome of the Bay Area "Funk" artist.

Toward the end of the sixties, Hudson began to reduce the complexity of his sculptures while at the same time increasing their bulk. Compared with work produced on either side of it, the sculpture produced between 1968 and 1972 has an austerity verging on the cerebral. Color itself plays a minor part in the work of this period as

Hudson explored further the ability of smooth-sheened or highly reflective surface textures to create spacial ambiguities. Within this short time frame and relatively limited body of work, two categories of sculpture can be discerned: one group, large, highly finished, room-consuming; the other, smaller "assemblage" pieces emphasizing the found object.

The large machinelike sculptures that Hudson produced around 1970 represent the most marked departure in his work from the characteristics outlined earlier. In them, Hudson concentrated on the potential of reflections alone to create illusory effects. Works such as *True Blue,* 1970 (cat. 21), or *Black Lift,* 1968 (cat. 16), pose relatively few tantalizing perceptual riddles, but, rather like the Minimalist sculpture of Donald Judd or Sol LeWitt, to which they have some kinship, Hudson's pieces of this period demand that the viewer simply accommodate their very existence. Yet, in common with all Hudson sculpture, they manage to be both assertive and puzzling: what they lack in color they make up for in size. There is little spatial ambiguity to them; their implied mystery derives from their technological appearance. Nowhere else in Hudson's oeuvre is the sense of the machine ethic so pervasive. *True Blue* literally looks like a piece of atomic equipment, and little imagination is necessary to see it in a laboratory or testing area. *Black Lift,* too, has space age connotations—a model for a satellite perhaps—made all the more feasible by the near industrial finish Hudson chose to give it. The artist's fastidious craftsmanship is a contributing factor to the personality of these mute, vaguely threatening works, and, in the context of the Minimalist movement that dominated these few years, it is worth noting that Hudson fabricates his own work which is not the case with most Minimalists. But the similarities between Hudson's work of this period and Minimalist sculpture are, after all, general rather than specific, and, above all, relative to the rest of Hudson's work. Place Hudson's "Minimalist" *True Blue* next to a truly Minimalist sculpture such as a Judd box, and *True Blue* suddenly seems very unminimal—positively loquacious, in fact.

The second group evolved from Hudson's awareness of Conceptual Art, the movement in which purely verbal and philosophical inquiries came close to banishing the "visual" from the "visual arts." *Stacked Deck* (p. 13) of 1972 consists of a pile of neoprene sheets neatly and tightly strapped to a dolly. On the top is a metal plate bearing the phrase "No Words." Hudson was typically amused that, in recording his lack of the use of words in making the piece, he *had* ended up using them after all. In *Still Works,* 1970 (cat. 20), Hudson presented his old, inexpensive welder, bought when he was a student, as a sculpture. The title has several meanings depending on whether "Still" is read as continues to, quiescent, or Clyfford Still (the Abstract Expressionist painter who exercised such a lasting influence on the art of the Bay Area). In part, the title reflects Hudson's amazement that the small welder is still in working condition after ten year's

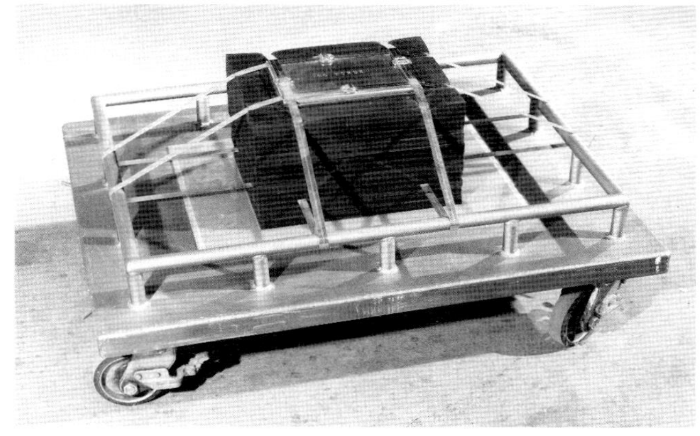

heavy use, but the final irony, of course, is that if the welder is presented as art, it cannot function as a tool, but that while quiescent as a manufacturing tool, it continues to work as a piece of art. Hudson's verbal ins and outs, the backwards and forwards of this title, are closely allied to his more familiar visual ambiguities.

In 1972, following this visually and conceptually austere period, Hudson did another about face and embarked upon a second collaborative project, this time with ceramicist Richard Shaw, that stretched almost two years. Hudson had long looked with envy on the ceramicist's malleable medium and expected to be able to work without the kind of ever present technical demands he encountered in welding steel. As Michael Schwager discusses in detail elsewhere in this book, such was not the case. Hudson found himself caught up in a new set of equally demanding procedures so that, when he returned to sculpture proper in 1974, his approach to it was markedly affected by his experience with ceramics.

Hudson had always incorporated found objects into his sculpture, but, in the work of the sixties, not only had their "non-art" origins been obscured by Hudson's practice of painting all surfaces, but the found objects— bent pipes, discarded metal fragments—were basically beat-up relatives of their welded neighbors. Even the elegant halo form floating at the center of *Inside Out*, 1964 (cat. 7), was actually a found object. While discussing this element, Hudson enlarged upon his attitude to found objects in general. He obtained three of these rings in 1964: "They're a really beautiful light metal," he says, "some kind of antennae of a ship." Such a find is not, it seems, to be used casually. "These things," he continues, "become so precious to me, so it has to be really worth it to use them up. I used one [in *Inside Out*], and the next time I used one was in *Hot Water*... nearly twenty years later... and the other one is leaning against the [studio] wall."

After his experience with ceramics, the found object emerged from hiding to assume a prominent position in much of his sculpture of the 1970s. Indeed welded forms virtually disappeared for a while as Hudson extended his range of forms and materials and basically employed an assemblage technique. Hudson himself uses the term "construction" to differentiate them from the predominantly welded work. In the 1974 *Cowboy Saddle Light* (cat. 26), a wide variety of objects including a cowboy hat, a stool, and a bowling ball hang from a branch set on a tripod; some surfaces are painted while others are left in their original state. The work has an informality bordering on the haphazard, and colors, particularly on the globelike shape, are broken and fugitive.

In another work, *Running through the Woods*, 1975 (p. 49), Hudson painted circles and angular patches directly onto the coat of the stuffed deer that is the startling focus of the construction. The paint disrupts the organic form of the animal but at the same time relates it to the gridlike base on which it stands. All manner of bits and pieces hang like talismans from the deer; its face is framed by a slender black-and-white rod in the shape of a triangle that hangs from the horns of the deer. Between the horns "floats" a globe pierced by the triangle. The piece evokes a sense of mystery and ritual. Confronted with elements that have such strong individual identities, there is a distinct inclination to ask why they are there, to read the work like a chart or map, seeking relationships between, say, the feathers that hang down from the black-and-white triangle and the identically colored spirals that dangle from the deer. Hudson himself does not altogether encourage this approach: his discussion of the work emphasizes that objects accrued as he resolved to make a sculpture out of the improbable and rather intractable starting point of a large stuffed animal. Looked at from this perspective, *Running through the Woods* is an essay in conflicting natural and geometric forms. On the other hand, there is no doubt that in the finished sculpture, the artist has given us something shamanistic, something permeated with hidden potent meaning, and, in this case, the impetus for the sculpture dates back a few years when he heard Jim McGrath recount an Indian ceremony in New Mexico during the course of which a dead deer was decorated by the participants.

At this time, Hudson was in step with a number of younger artists who, in the mid-seventies, reacted against the abstract inscrutability of Minimalism in favor of work with highly charged and often narrative content. Autobiography, ritual, and mythology were favorite subjects as artists delineated fanciful life histories for themselves and others, or attempted to tap into the ineffable myths of remote civilizations. Wiley, for example, was a leading figure in this movement, having evolved a highly personal, deliberately unheroic but intensely poetic, mode of working that drew inspiration from his day-to-day surroundings in Marin County, California.

Hudson never went that far, but the newfound autonomy of the found object contributed to the generally autobiographical feel of his work at this time, and, though generally only implicit, in at least one work, *Daddy's Apron Strings*, 1976 (cat. 29), it is made explicit. The title plays on the taunt, "Mommy's apron strings," but the apron is that of a carpenter, the occupation of Hudson's father. By using the apron as a canvas, painting on it complex illusionistic space, and adorning it with all manner of things, Hudson makes ironic reference to his own daily chore of making art. The decorated apron signifies his craft while being a work of art itself. From the bottom of the apron hangs an ambiguous hank of hair, a visual pun that can be read as a whisk brush or pony tail, a phallic element, or even a scalp.

Further references to Indian art and ritual are found in *Kachina* (p. 15), another 1976 wall-mounted construction that deals with aspects of order and chaos. The title refers to the little doll in the piece Hudson made from a whisk broom that, in color at least, has similarities with the Kachina dolls of the Hopi and Pueblo Indians. The doll is suspended from a long steel rod which, when pulled down and released, causes the multijointed doll to dance frenziedly. Viewed from the front, the rod appears to emanate from an arrangement of globes and discs that resembles a solar system. A real globe juxtaposed against the multicolored child's basketball at the center of the "system" encourages reading the random pattern in the ball as land and water masses. Correspondingly, the arbitrary colors of the basketball tend to highlight the arbitrary nature of the colors used by the mapmaker. A fanned-out book of carefully graduated stain samples hinting at order project from the shelf below the "system" as if in orbit. A wooden ruler, painted with the colors of the light spectrum, suggests that the whole thing can be somehow quantified. In an opposing spirit, the very random form of a rock hangs down bearing the words "So Long," which can be taken as either a very imprecise measurement, a casual farewell, or a vague span of time.

By the end of the decade, Hudson had moved back to working exclusively with welded and painted steel, and, in recent work, Hudson has again tended to subordinate the found object to his abiding interest in real and illusory space. Even so, in a number of works a wide variety of such things as antlers, cast-iron dogs, and branches fulfill a significant role by accentuating or acting as a foil to the increasingly intricate fabricated elements. In *Balance Point*, 1982 (cat. 35), for example, the rhythmic forms of the horns and antlers complement the exquisite steel arabesques, while their natural grain texture is echoed in delicately striated colors that Hudson applied with pastel sticks.

Plumb Bob, 1982 (p. 61), and its close relative of the same year, *Hot Water* (p. 16), represent Hudson's first deliberate (if not exactly unequivocal) creations of a figure. The stick figures are, in a sense, autobiographical. Not only does the title of one refer directly to Hudson's given name, but both of these stick figures dangle eye-fooling geometric devices of the kind found in so much of his sculpture. Of these devices, a particular favorite has been the necker cube that has been compressed, as it were, by pressure on two opposing corners.[2] It occurs in many guises: sometimes solid, sometimes only three-sided, and on yet other occasions as the painted illusion of it. Similarly, the geodesic feature in *Plumb Bob* can be located in various forms in earlier works such as *Black Lift*, 1968 (cat. 16). However, it should be clear by now that Hudson is no theoretician, scientifically examining every aspect of a given problem. His use of geometry is wholly intuitive, an attitude perfectly illustrated by his

2. Necker cube: an ambiguous figure. A situation is set up in which the eye is given two sets of perspectives and is unable to make a choice between the two.

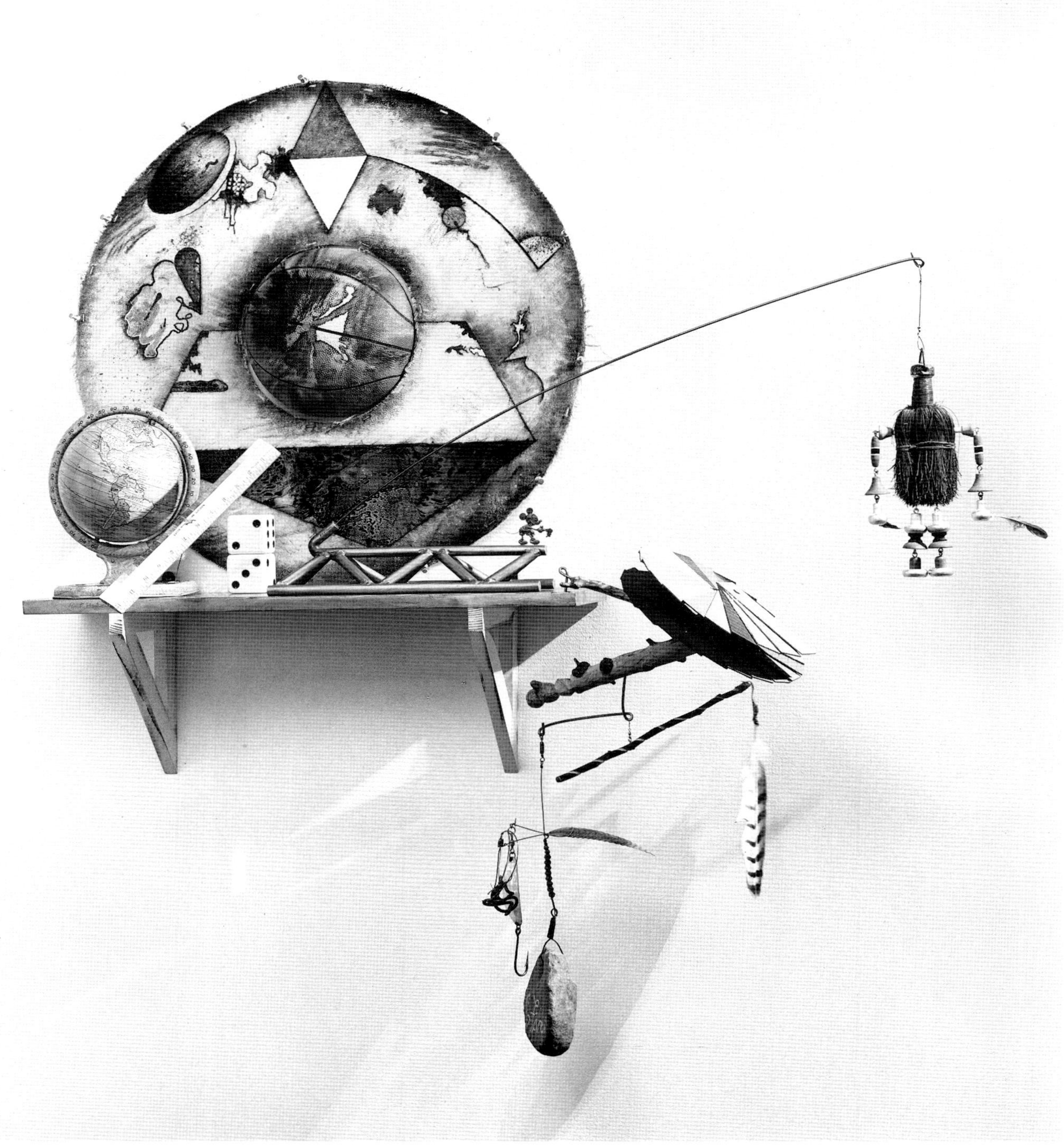

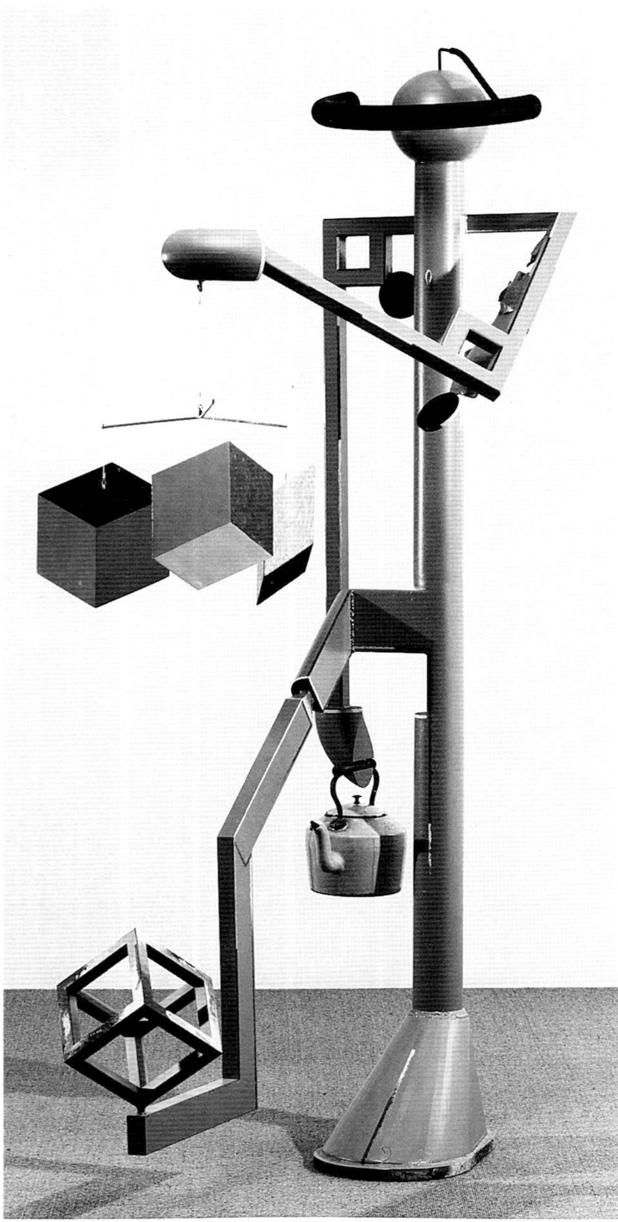

response to the open cube that balances at an angle on one foot of *Hot Water.* "The cube spins," he says, "and then it does weird things; it makes a kind of curve.... Those outside points blend into a perfect half-circle. I couldn't figure out how it worked.... It's bizarre, magic; but I don't know if I *want* to figure it out."

"Figuring out" *Steel Kachina* (cat. 44), also from 1982, is relatively straightforward. A solid-steel doll figure with a Pinocchio nose and beady black eyes is shadowed by an amorphous wire figure. Both figures are intersected by an angular metal strip whose placement seems arbitrary but, when seen from one angle, snaps into focus as a near perfect square. Hudson frequently employs this sort of occurrence, whether accidental or painstakingly contrived, to inject surprise and delight into his work. He personally derives profound pleasure from the fact that the legs and splayed feet of the steel Kachina are "made out of two hearts, perfect hearts split and bent—just folded," and that its zigzag lightning headdress is made from the elements cut away from the solid body. Without the artist's words on this, there would be little to indicate such disciplined use of materials particularly as all the artist's effort in this direction is subsumed into sculptures that teeter on the edge of pure chaos. Atypically, *Steel Kachina* is unpainted. Hudson liked the "lush looking metal" and limited his brush to the zigzag. Even here the colors— gray, white, beige and yellow—are muted.

In all other works, Hudson's painted surfaces have reached an unparalleled degree of complexity. Those of the seven-foot-high *Untitled,* 1983 (p. 64), change hue and texture almost inch by inch, varying from dappled reds and blues to areas of solid greens, purples, and oranges. In a passage reminiscent of earlier work, Hudson painted a black-and-white wedge onto an elliptical form so that, from one aspect, the passage flattens out into the corner of a square the rest of which is formed by the main frame of the sculpture. As he has always done, he treats two- and three-dimensional surfaces as if they were interchangeable and, through his artistic act of will, makes it seem as if they are.

As has already been remarked, Hudson's inclusive attitude toward materials and his persistent use of all the means at his disposal make his work susceptible to elaborate and sometimes fanciful interpretation. Hudson himself has strong feelings about certain shapes and particular objects which he uses with a full sense of their history, personal or artistic, but, if there is a "message" in his sculpture, it is general rather than specific. The final resolution that Hudson gives to each sculpture, for all its illusion and questioning of space, is curiously positive. Each work asserts, somehow, the pleasure of forms, objects, textures, colors, and, by implication, the glory of the many varied things that surround us. It is perhaps a culminating irony of Hudson's work that it so consistently gives voice to the very unmodernist notion that, when all is said and done, more is—well—actually more.

Casting Illusions: The Ceramics of Robert Hudson

by Michael Schwager

Robert Hudson's ceramics represent not only a transitional period between his large, monochromatic sculptures of the early 1970s and the more complex and colorful paintings, drawings, and sculptures of the mid-1970s and beyond, but they are also a distinct and fully realized body of work in a medium previously unfamiliar to him. The works in porcelain, produced between 1971 and 1974, reflect the technical virtuosity and exacting craftsmanship Hudson displayed in his earlier welded-steel and painted-steel sculptures. In addition, the jars, bottles, cups, and teapots Hudson devoted himself to during this time renewed an earlier interest in both found objects and richly painted surfaces that would affect his work in other media for years to follow.

To fully understand the porcelain work of Robert Hudson, one must first examine both the circumstances surrounding Hudson's temporary departure from steel sculpture and his close personal friendship and professional collaboration with artist Richard Shaw.

By the fall of 1971, Hudson had been welding and painting heavy pieces of steel for over ten years. The sculptures of 1968 to 1971 had become more contained and linear, increasing in size at the same time the range and intensity of their surface color were being diminished. It has been observed that, for Hudson, there may have been "a kind of loss in them; loss in terms of immediacy and scale."[1] Hudson began to feel that he was ready for a change in both the medium and direction of his work. He hoped to find "something that was equally satisfying and a lot friendlier" than steel.[2] He had long been aware of the many artists in the Bay Area working in clay. James Melchert and Ron Nagle were teaching at the San Francisco Art Institute while Hudson was a student there, and he later joined Nagle, Melchert, and Peter Voulkos on the art department faculty of the University of California, Berkeley. Hudson truly admired the work of these artists, along with other ceramic sculptors such as Robert Arneson and Kenneth Price, and was drawn to the apparent speed with which they were able to develop their ideas in clay.

More tired esthetically than physically with working in steel, Hudson discussed his desire to explore different materials and methods of working with his friend Richard Shaw. The two had known one another since Hudson was Shaw's senior sculpture instructor at the San Francisco Art Institute in 1965. In 1967, Shaw and his family joined Hudson at a ranch in Stinson Beach, California, that was conveniently equipped with two separate houses and facilities for two studios as well. Their friendship deepened as they proceeded to make art and raise children in close proximity to each other.

In September 1971, Hudson and Shaw agreed to embark on a project in which both artists would work together in Shaw's studio using porcelain as their primary means of expression. For Shaw, it meant moving away from the hand-built objects in earthenware he had been making since the late 1960s.[3] Although he had worked with porcelain for the first time just several months earlier while a visiting artist at the University of Wisconsin, Madison, he was thoroughly familiar with other materials and techniques associated with ceramic sculpture. Hudson's only previous experience with clay, on the other hand, was two ceramic sculpture classes he took while an undergraduate in art school. The change in technique, materials, and scale he would encounter working in porcelain proved to be anything but disappointing: "I liked working small. It all fitted: the time, the clay, the speed, the scale."

Indeed, the move to porcelain seemed perfectly suited to each of the artist's sensibilities. Both Hudson and Shaw were interested in using porcelain to express painterly and sculptural concerns, much as Voulkos and his colleagues John Mason and Price had begun to do over a decade earlier at the Otis Art Institute in Los Angeles (now the Otis Art Institute of Parsons School of Design).[4] The fact that porcelain, when fired, is nonporous and therefore eliminates the need for a shiny, vitreous glaze, along with the relative ease with which it can be thinned for use in slip casting, made it an obvious choice. The stark white surface of porcelain lent itself to the painting Hudson would once again so thoroughly involve himself with, and the thin, almost translucent quality of high-fired porcelain was compatible with the type of complex assemblages he would build with cast and wheel-thrown shapes.

As the project began, Hudson soon learned that the speed with which he hoped to produce complete works in porcelain was not immediately forthcoming. Unfamiliar with many of the techniques he would need to employ, he was at first dependent on Shaw for advice on everything from the formulas for mixing slip to the proper temperatures for firing the finished pieces. The artists' decision to work primarily with cast objects also slowed their initial progress.

Using found objects gathered from around the studio or discovered during their frequent trips to second-hand stores in San Francisco and Marin County, Hudson and Shaw set about making molds of plastic toys, buckets, rocks, bottles, and twigs. To fabricate the molds, they first poured casting plaster around an object that had been set into a block of clay. A wooden box was then built

1. Jan Butterfield, *Robert Hudson* (New York: Allan Frumkin Gallery, 1976): n.p.

2. All quotations not otherwise credited are taken from Robert Hudson's remarks during interviews with the author in February 1985.

3. Richard Marshall and Suzanne Foley, *Ceramic Sculpture: Six Artists* (Seattle and London: University of Washington Press in association with the Whitney Museum of American Art, 1981): 120.

4. Two excellent sources of information on the development of contemporary American ceramics are: Garth Clark and Margie Hughto, *A Century of Ceramics in the United States 1878-1978* (New York: E.P. Dutton in association with the Everson Museum of Art, 1979); and Rose Slivka, "The New Ceramic Presence," *Craft Horizons* (July-August 1961): 31-37.

around the clay to contain the plaster. This was repeated on the other half of the object, resulting in one complete mold of two sections. Some of the more complex objects they used required casting in three or more different molds. Once the molds were completed, registration keys were added to each half to assure that they would fit tightly together and in the same direction. A shaft was hollowed out along the center of the mold, and slip, basically liquid clay, was poured in. The clay body had been deflocculated, or thinned out, with sodium silicate, making it more fluid and thus usable in plaster casts. In the final stages of slip casting, excess moisture was pulled from the porcelain slip by the plaster mold. As the clay wall thickened, the rest of the slip was poured out. The mold was then opened and the hollow cast piece removed.[5]

Hudson and Shaw made literally hundreds of molds. As Shaw has noted, "We reached a point where we would begin to see things as two- or three-part molds.... Everything became a potential object we could cast."[6] The cast objects and shapes were spread onto a large table in the studio and covered with sheets of plastic to keep the porcelain from drying out. Along with some traditional shapes such as cylinders that Shaw threw on a potter's wheel and forms that were hand-built from either slabs or coils of porcelain, the cast pieces became part of a large inventory of found objects to be used by both artists.

Fully aware of the long history of porcelain in the production of functional pottery, Hudson began using traditional ceramic shapes as points of departure from which his pieces would evolve. Having never made pottery before, Hudson genuinely enjoyed the concept of making a complex piece of sculpture that could also function as a teapot or bottle. The idea of functional sculpture was something Hudson had also come across in the Mayan ceramics of ninth-century Mexico. Although Hudson had most likely been aware of this work for some time, among the many books and magazines that passed through the Stinson Beach studio were several volumes on Mayan ceramics. Hudson remembers being impressed by the "bottles and jars that were also figures and heads. They made these beautiful sculptures that were also used for pouring and storing things. They even made these pots that somehow whistled as you poured from them."

First choosing molds of bowls, spheres, bottles, and other shapes that could conceivably function as containers, Hudson began to assemble teapots, jars, and cups, adding cast objects as the works progressed. The traditional vessels would begin to look like composites of seemingly unrelated shapes and forms that at times completely obscured the intended functions of the pieces. In *Teapot*, 1972 (p. 41), what appears to be a strange landscape of petrified trees and floating globes on an otherwise barren planet is actually just what the title suggests.

The bent twig that juts out from the central branch is also the spout. The larger of the two spheres serves as the lid and can be removed to reveal the mouth of the teapot. The section of a tree branch that is attached to the body of the pot can be used as a handle for pouring.

Hudson took the implied function of his ceramics seriously. The connections between each of the separate elements are hollow, allowing a smooth flow of liquids. He even applied a clear glaze to the inside of all the ceramics, although it was technically not necessary since "porcelain is almost completely vitreous, like glass. The glaze just added to that idea of being functional. If you made a cup, and it wasn't glazed on the inside, it would be rough and strange to use. It just seemed like I should add that layer of glaze."

Once the completed form was dried and bisque fired, Hudson started applying color to the surface of the porcelain. Avoiding the loud colors and glossy finish of standard earthenware, he painted water-based underglazes directly onto the porcelain. The underglazes were absorbed into the clay, softening the colors and giving the piece a matte finish. Hudson used both standard paintbrushes and an airbrush to apply the color, enabling him to achieve a variety of surface textures. In some pieces, such as *Teapot*, 1973 (p. 22), the surfaces were developed as independent, yet related, illusionistic paintings. Hudson borrowed patterns such as checkerboards, stars, and circles from his welded-steel sculptures of the early 1960s. The areas of color, much softer than those Hudson used in the past, still served to contradict the shape and volume of the forms instead of emphasize them, creating a dynamic tension between the illusion of the painting and the structure of the object.

In other works, the various cast elements were painted with such startling realism that it is difficult at times to tell them from the real thing. Hudson spent hours recreating the color and texture of a single twig or stone. These trompe l'oeil pieces reinforce the surrealist overtones found in Hudson's work, encouraging the viewer to consider the different elements as real objects with functions and associations quite separate from their incorporation into a work of art. For Hudson, the juxtaposition of these incongruous objects was as much a formal consideration as anything else. He used the porcelain casts "first as a shape, then as a branch or a rock. I was interested in putting different colors and shapes together, seeing how they would react to each other."

Hudson began to incorporate actual objects into his ceramic work, using strips of leather, pieces of tree branch, and even a quartz crystal, as in *Bottle*, 1973 (p. 21). This use of found objects, while appearing to have developed concurrently with the ceramics, actually dates back to some of the sculptures he made as a student. He abandoned this device as he became more involved with steel, only to rediscover it with the works in porcelain. Hudson's use

5. Suzanne Foley, *Robert Hudson/Richard Shaw: Work in Porcelain* (San Francisco: San Francisco Museum of Art, 1973): 3.

6. Richard Shaw in conversation with the author, 19 February 1985, Fairfax, California.

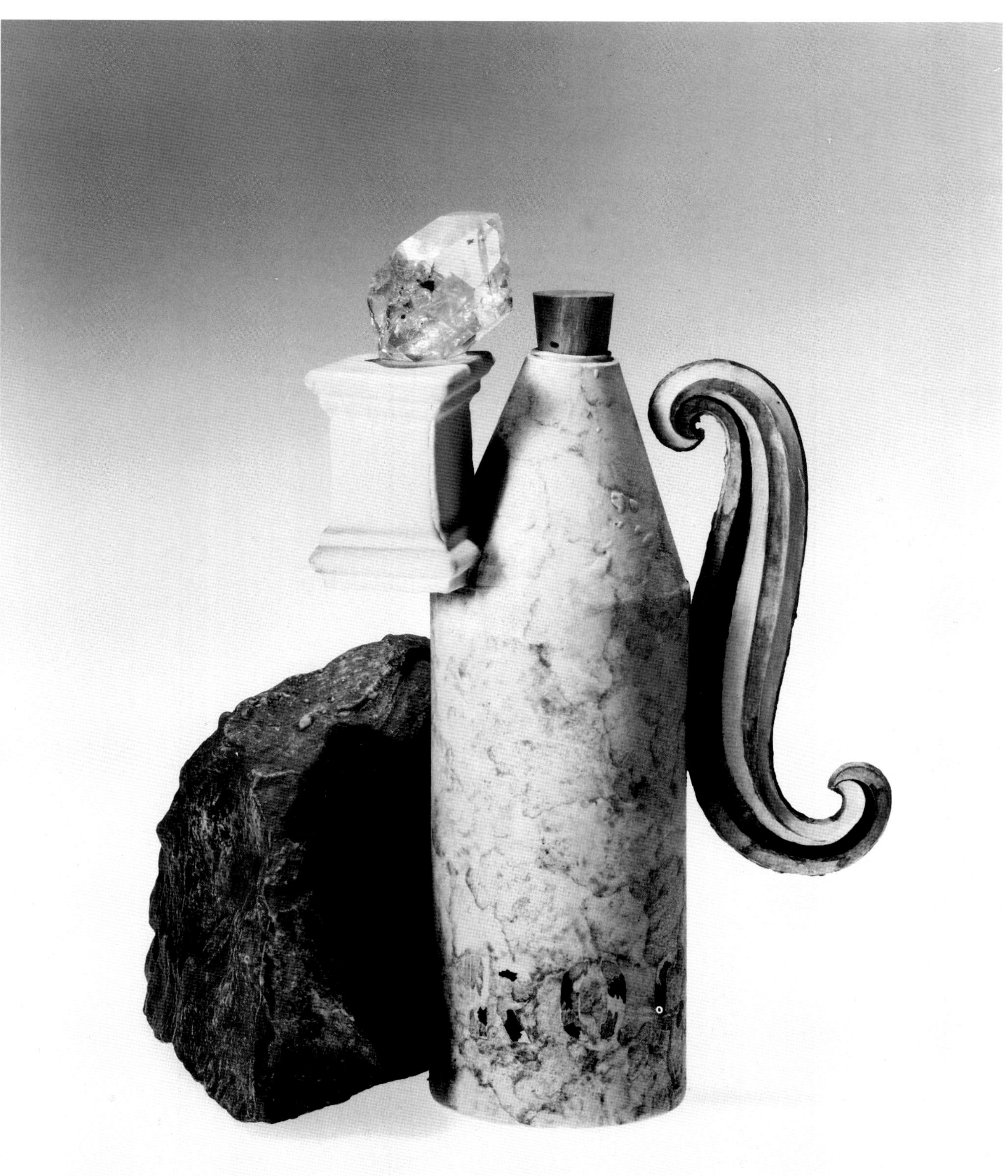

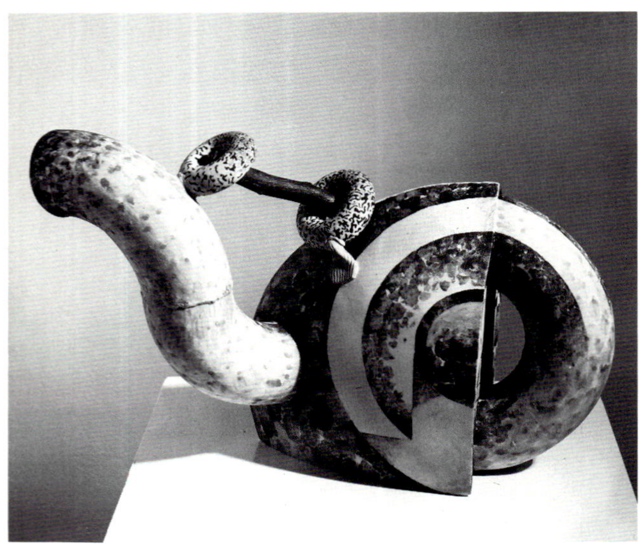

of actual found objects not only further blurred the distinctions between what was real and what was porcelain, but also influenced his approach to the assemblage sculpture he began to make shortly after he started working with Shaw.

Bowl, 1973 (p. 40), is an example of Hudson's use of both real and cast objects, and is one of his most sculptural works in porcelain. The bottom portion of the work consists of a bowl shape that Hudson cast from a plastic bucket, then placed on a potter's wheel to turn down the edge, creating a smooth lip for the bowl. The central, vertical element is a cast section of fence post that appears as if it were used to support other objects while they were being painted. On one side of the post, a cast piece of lumber rests on the lip of the bowl and supports an unusual arrangement of carved sticks and architectural elements, all made of porcelain. The architectural details were cast from molds Hudson and Shaw found in the studio they moved to in Sausalito during the late fall of 1972. To one of these sticks is tied a piece of fluorescent string on the end of which dangles a small star. Out of the other side of the post jut two porcelain pegs. A short length of leather connects one of the pegs with a section of a real tree branch. This work invites repeated examination not only because of the somewhat confusing mixture of real and cast objects, but also because of its size and the complexity of its composition. Its thrust and movement, along with the precarious balance of some of the elements, is directly related to the sculptures that follow the ceramics.

In addition to the underglazes, Hudson used oil-based china paints to decorate the porcelains. The china paints—brilliant reds, oranges, and sky blues—gave Hudson a greater range of the bright colors he sometimes used. In *Cup,* 1972 (p. 40), one of the earliest ceramics in the exhibition, most of its surface is covered with china paint. The work is unusually glossy due to the application of a clear glaze to the porcelain's surface prior to adding the china paint. The overall pattern of the decoration consists of interlocking biomorphic and geometric shapes, outlined in black and filled in with shades of yellow, orange, blue, and red, which recall the watercolors of Hudson's longtime friend William T. Wiley.

As Hudson continued working on the ceramics, he began to experience once again the joy of painting he had so fully expressed in the steel sculptures of nearly a decade before. The colors assumed a more softened sense. The details became more intricate; the patterns more abstract. Perhaps one of the most remarkable examples of Hudson's painterly treatment of the ceramics is *Jar,* 1972-73 (p. 40). A familiar collection of cast objects has been united in a fairly compact configuration. The main portion of the jar was made from a cast of an old-fashioned glass fishbowl, on top of which sits another of the cast, dough-nut-shaped plastic toys Hudson used in several of the porcelains. A shape that can be read as a handle is actually a porcelain cast of a standard steel elbow found in many of Hudson's sculptures. On what might be seen as the front of the piece, a group of porcelain twigs seems to defy gravity, floating up from the surface of the jar. The tallest twig is crowned by four black-and-white cone shapes cast from paper Dixie cups. The twigs have been treated with Hudson's usual keen attention to detail, but, for the first time, we also find a strikingly realistic, two-dimensional painting of the twigs on the same side of the jar. Hudson seems to be calling attention to the multiple levels of reality his found objects are endowed with, as in the aforemen-tioned *Bottle* (p. 21), in which he used a real rock (the quartz crystal), a cast rock, and the printed word "rock" on the side of the bottle.

The rest of the jar is painted with atmospheric fields of pastel colors. Abstract forms float across the sur-face, creating the illusion of depth as the shapes move in front of and behind one another. Black lines simulating cracks in the porcelain add to the spatial illusions. The minute details are many, including the artist's signature and date of the piece, carefully written across a cast ball-point pen that rests atop the jar. The surface of the jar reads like a three-dimensional abstract painting on a small scale. In fact, Hudson has stated on several occasions that it was ceramics such as this one that led him to begin the paintings and drawings dating from 1973.

As with the work of any artist who uses recog-nizable objects that possess a separate meaning outside of their formal or symbolic associations, Hudson's ceram-ics have been subject to a variety of interpretations. Much has been made of Hudson's "autobiographical" use of nat-ural objects, such as twigs, deer hooves, and rocks, along with references to the American cowboy and Native American mythology. In a work such as *Indian Pot,* 1973 (p. 40), these symbols abound: sections of a tree branch, a deer's hoof, beads and feathers, and even a cast profile similar to the one found on an Indian head nickel. Since Hudson grew up in a rural section of Washington state near an Indian reservation, and lived much of his adult life in the many pastoral parts of the San Francisco Bay Area, it is reasonable to assume that this has certainly influenced Hudson's choice of imagery in his work. It is even safer to assume, however, that any autobiographical references are more subconscious rather than direct attempts at self-portraiture, for Hudson is an acute observer of his environ-ment, both immediate and beyond. He retains images he finds meaningful, either intellectually or formally, and processes them through his own highly personal sensibility. The images then surface in his work when the right set of circumstances have arisen. It is this unique vision that in part gives Hudson's work its distinction and strength.

The project that was to last "only two or three months" became an intense period of work that contin-ued for over two years in two separate studios, culminat-ing in two separate exhibitions.[7] Robert Hudson's work in porcelain broadened not only his own visual vocabulary, but generated much excitement in both the fine art and crafts communities. The ceramics are playful and imagina-tive, elegant and surreal. They have both expanded the concept of the functional ceramic object and added another chapter to the history of contemporary ceramic sculpture.

7. The first exhibition was at the San Francisco Museum of Art (now the San Francisco Museum of Modern Art) in 1973. Hudson and Shaw each exhibited forty-nine works dating from 1971 to 1973. The second show was at the E.G. Gallery (now the Dorry Gates Gallery) in Kansas City, Missouri. Most of the approximately twenty works by each artist were from late 1973 and 1974, and are considered by the artists to be "a separate group" from the works shown in San Francisco.

Perceptual Alchemy: The Paintings of Robert Hudson

by Jan Butterfield

Now think of hands and eyes:
ceremonial masks
spider web charms
the four directions
winter count figures
eagle feathers
circles of sun and heart
bear claws
hand prints on stones
pictomyths of feeling
eyes of woodland dolls
wind in the trees
rhythm

*Now whistle on the wind and touch your eyes four times
with your hands while you listen to these stories about
seeing and knowing.*[1]

Robert Hudson's paintings are so elusive that, viewing them, one is not sure, then *is* sure then is not sure again. Are they primitive, naïve images culled up from the wellspring of the unconscious, or sophisticated renderings with a long art historical heritage? Are their curious signs and symbols meaningful images from this culture, this life, or are they put there for some other reason not fully defined or understood? Shaping with paint, building trompe l'oeil images across his surfaces, lyrically, seductively plying his magic, slyly manipulating perceptual phenomena, Hudson often speaks in visual tongues. Rippling and tangling his colors across the surface of a work, he creates glorious visual enigmas: "The thing I like...is making flat things go round with paint. Just being able to have an object be what it is and then also be something else—like a whisper or a dance."[2]

Hudson's recent works are an amalgamation of abstract and representational images: primitive magic objects such as feathers, rawhide, string, beads, sticks, rocks, carved twigs and branches, and collaged photographs which co-mingle with exquisitely painted arcs, circles, and triangles and volumes and globes. He acknowledges a debt to Vasily Kandinsky, and also to Henri Matisse. Will Grohmann's definitive book on Kandinsky was on a studio table the first time I visited Hudson's studio in the late 1970s. I was immediately struck with a curious sense of confirmation—there were rich and interesting parallels between Kandinsky's works in the 1912 to 1914 period and the work Hudson was then doing. More recently there is a brushy lyricism that also seems to faintly echo Matisse. There are also contemporary parallels with Robert Rauschenberg, Jasper Johns, and with the more recent work of Frank Stella, but those parallels

are only kinship, not influence, for Hudson's work resembles nothing so much as itself. A bravura explosion of color and form, its roots go deeply into the Bay Area figurative tradition, and the unique brand of Abstract Expressionism practiced there in the "Golden Era" of the 1940s and 1950s. Hudson has more in common with cronies such as William T. Wiley, William Allan, Robert Arneson, Manuel Neri, and Joan Brown than he does with any historical European figure or with any East Coast artist. It is to those figures, each of whom has carved out a distinct niche in the history of contemporary art, that one must look for true colleagueship and/or influence. Hudson is a kind of movement unto himself. He is also the archetypal Bay Area artist, as Peter Schjeldahl has noted:

"Robert Hudson...by himself might appear practically archetypal of the Bay Area artist....Hudson's work in construction, ceramics, collage painting, drawing and whatnot mediums is certainly various enough, and there's no gainsaying the 'eccentricity' of his images. However, Hudson is also extremely sophisticated in his eclecticism, with a kind of sophistication that tends to elude New York tastes precisely because it includes and exceeds them."[3]

Hudson's studio provides clues which aid in the untangling of the rich visual puzzle that makes up his art. The studio is situated in the rural countryside of Cotati, a small town in Northern California. Like most of his Bay Area colleagues, Hudson prefers to live in the country. Here a field of new spring grass separates the house from the studio, and the wind whistles and rustles through a stand of Eucalyptus trees which are part of the property. The studio was newly built when Hudson moved to Cotati in 1977, but it quickly acquired the patina of use and accumulation. Everywhere objects are waiting to be revivified. A taxidermic deer's head with full antlers hangs on the wall next to a huge stuffed bird with its wings outstretched. These creatures keep company with three skeletons purchased from a medical supply house. Hanging from the ceiling is a curtain of glass beads—its stylized tropical fish coy, almost living companions to the inert deer and skeletons. Rusty toys and implements with intriguing shapes are scattered about, waiting to be chosen. An oversized beer can hangs from the ceiling.

Historically it is probably to Kurt Schwitters and then to Johns and Rauschenberg that one can look regarding Hudson's penchant for assemblage which permeates the paintings and the works on paper, as well as the three-dimensional works. In virtually all his assemblage works, Hudson combines the old, the used, and the fragmented to create a gentle poetry with perceptual twists and turns. He includes the strange, odd, and bizarre objects that find their way to him, as well as powerful images from his own reservoir: feathers, beads, wire, string, and old paper fans

1. Gerald Vizenor, "Tribal People and the Poetic Image: Visions of Eyes and Hands," from *American Indian Form and Tradition* (Minneapolis: Walker Art Center, 1972).

2. Unless otherwise noted, all quotes are from Robert Hudson in conversation with the author.

3. Peter Schjeldahl, *Robert Hudson* (Philadelphia: Moore College of Art Gallery, 1978), p. 7.

are juxtaposed with seed packets, images from herbal
tea boxes, and envelopes of frozen peas. All of these are
overpainted, supported, or fleshed out with rich color
and shapes and enhanced by Hudson's own wiry calligraphy drawn and/or brushed on with astonishing vivacity
and energy. For all their lushness, the works are sure and
crisp. There appear to be no erasures, corrections, or
overworked areas. The artist moves quickly, and with great
facility, from one area to another. Above all, it is a body
of work that stuns, not only because it is good—and you
immediately sense that—but also because Hudson makes
it look so easy.

There is also another aspect to Hudson, and that
is the man who understands the trees in the forest, the
animals, and the soul in rocks. Raised near the Yakima
Indian reservation in Washington, Hudson has had a close
intuitive link with Indian life and tradition since he was
a child. While his spiritual links with Indian tradition mani-
fest themselves most notably in his sculptures and assemblages, there are metaphors and refrains that run through
the paintings and drawings as well.

The historical and the intuitive make a chewy
mix. In the final analysis we find that Hudson's works are
so extraordinary and unique that ultimately art historical comparisons make weak parallels, and we are left
to struggle with the power and the beauty of the works
on our own—which a closer examination of the work
will indicate.

The Paintings

The singularity of Hudson's painting often begins
with the ground itself. One of the earliest paintings in
the exhibition, *Untitled III,* 1973 (p. 42), is a case in point.
A softened blur of pistachio and lilac, this painting is a green
cheese moon upon which the purple haze of infinity
appears to be reflected. One of a number of paintings
Hudson has executed on cotton batting, it has a rich surface quality that is without sheen and which posesses the
luminosity of pastels.

Cotton batting is curious material. Firmly
overstitched with gridding, which gives it a kind of faux
formalism, its look and feel belie its modest beginnings
as padding for ironing board covers. Hudson bought great
rolls of the material, and had it around the studio for some
time before he cut it up and began to use it as canvas.
At that point in time, sometime in 1973, the artist had
been engaged for a year and a half in a serious round
of rather remarkable ceramic sculpture created with
assemblage techniques. The overpainting on those porous
porcelains took on a softened, pastel sensibility. It seemed
a natural jump from there to the softened surface of the
cotton batting—a seductive material which absorbs much
of the paint like a wick and leaves only a gentle color
on the surface. In reality, this jump was bigger than

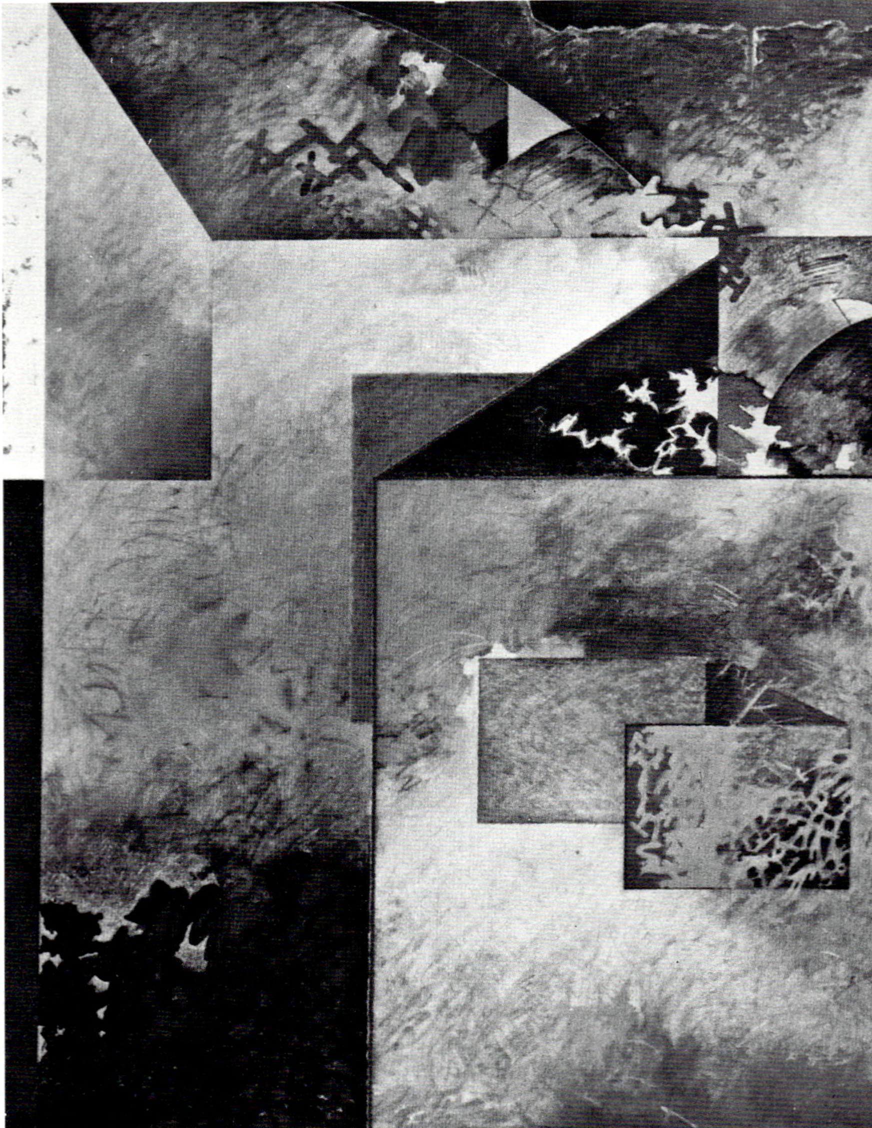

it seemed, for the artist had not painted since his student
days at the San Francisco Art Institute and somehow the
nontraditional aspect of the material allowed him to segue
with finesse from ceramics to painting, with scarcely
a beat in between.

Among the paintings created the first year of his
return to painting was *Love Lock,* 1974 (cat. 53), which paid
its respects to the beginnings of modernism. In this work,
Paul Cézanne's peaches rest coyly on a tabletop, the folds
of which are supported by richly painted triangles straight
out of Kandinsky. This painting also engages in a kind
of perceptual sleight-of-hand, for, like the mirrored images
in a kaleidoscope, the work feels as if it will momentarily
wink and shift—leaving its historical images behind as only
as fleeting memory.

Moving backwards in time from the historical
to the primitive, *Bear Claw,* 1976 (p. 46), is a very different
kind of painting. Here, in an undifferentiated blue haze and

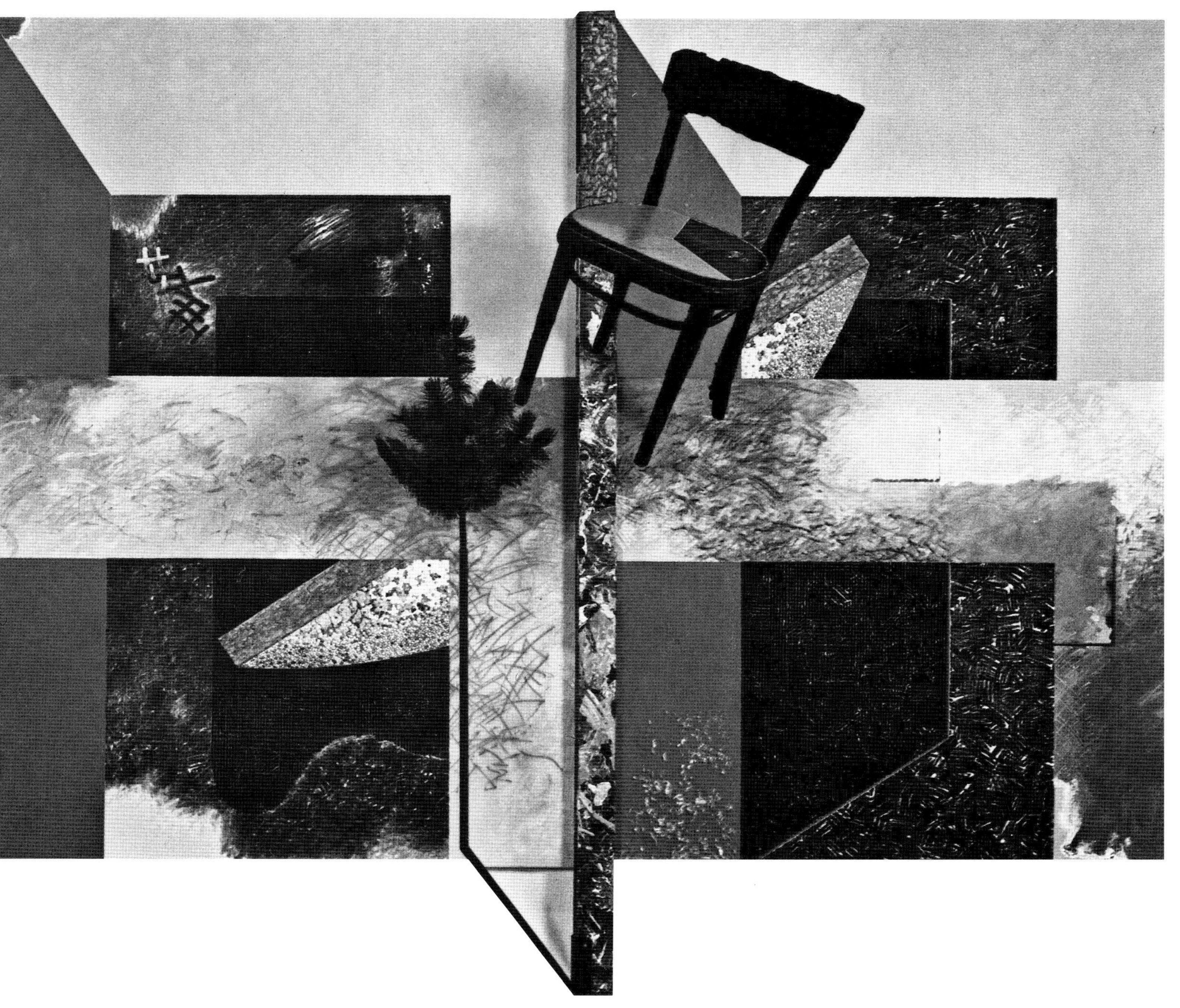

a thick cluster of cumulous clouds, the paw of a great white polar bear—the medicine man's magic, the magic of "The Spirit in the Sky"—emerges thrusting outwards toward the viewer, only the claws on its toes fully visible. Below, a cluster of symbols and images—like those on decorated rawhides—seems to emerge along the side of some strange architectural structure. This work is both sure in its own voice, and rich in its painterly qualities. Hudson the sculptor has moved comfortably into painting in a short period of time with great assurance.

Re-engaging himself with painting, Hudson quickly found his stride and created assemblage paintings which are among the most extraordinary works he has ever produced. Notable among these is *K-6*, 1977 (p. 44), which is thirteen feet long and almost seven feet high. This tour de force gives both Rauschenberg and Johns a run for their money, and rivals the off-the-wall works by Stella which were being done at that same time.

In *K-6*, what begins on the left as a painting takes shape as a collage in the center, and then finishes grandly as a fragmented sculptural assemblage on the right. Here, in an exquisite balance and counterbalance of shapes, colors, and objects, Hudson comes powerfully into his own as a painter. While one senses or feels historical roots firmly reaching back to Schwitters, that only grounds the work. Most specifically it derives its essence from the fertility of Hudson's talent and his uncanny visual repertoire.

On the left, an architectural shape, rather splendidly defined in brilliant yellow against clear red, is swirled around with a triple-curved rainbowed moebius strip, which snakes at an angle across the surface. In the center, against a ground of brushy blue, a round back wooden chair, ablaze with primary colors—red, yellow, and green against the blue—is echoed in shadow by the reality of the actual chair with its dull, ordinary brown surface making it appear as only a ghost of its vibrant painted self.

On the far right, the last third of the work appears to chip off like blocks of ice breaking away from an ice flow. Here, the once solid image now shatters, splinters, and breaks up—leaving empty spaces as poignant voids to play off crowded spaces filled with colorful strings, beads, coils, broken grids, and a shattered half of a wooden boat. Along with his sculpture *Running through the Woods*, 1975 (p. 49), which entangles a hundred years of art history via sign and symbol with a huge stuffed deer, and the assemblage *Daddy's Apron Strings*, 1976 (cat. 29), which turns an ordinary carpenter's apron into a poetic painter's device, *K-6* is one of Hudson's most magnificent works to date. Another assemblage work, *Spur of the Moment*, 1977 (cat. 61), is an example of Hudson at his imaginative best. Here a magic circle encloses powerful imagery: a convex mirror reflects a golden hand holding a paintbrush; a multicolored fishing creel hangs off to the side. From the central composition hangs beads which are also looped around

a rainbowed mixing stick supporting a galvanized tin bucket that reaches far beyond the painting to the floor below. The entire work is "framed" with canvas strapping "zigzags"; below, on the right, stretching off the wall and into the viewer's space, is a single silver spur from which the painting takes its title.

Another major painting is *Out of the Blue*, 1980-81 (p. 26). Here, "out of the blue"—literally—comes an unfolding panoply of multicolored and curious forms like a child's cut-out paper house, behind the windows of which can be seen fragmented elements of the cosmos. A jumble of twisted wire, a brown wooden chair, and a green plastic Christmas tree—as unlikely a collection of images and symbols as one could possibly imagine—are affixed to the front of the work. The final fillip is a confetti-spattered two-by-four which echoes a painted bar on the left. With the real board, however, the movement is off the canvas and onto the wall below the work. Clearly Hudson is moving at full force in the paintings by this period of time, and their combined improbability and assurance merge to create works of great power and innovation.

The Works on Paper

The primary difference between the works on canvas (or cotton batting) and the works on paper is their size—and the fact that the works on paper tend to have collaged elements because assemblage is largely impossible on a smaller scale. The works on paper continue the improbable juxtapositions found in the large-scale works. In one of the strangest, Untitled, 1977 (cat. 80), the work is essentially an uneven diptych, divided roughly two-thirds/one-third. This work is more ordered and formal than some of the others, yet Hudson's work, for all of its curious imagery, is very formal throughout. Here the sense of balance is impeccable. Its imagery is both abstract and literal. Two large collaged skeletons—placed against a vertical ground of brushy blue on the left and thick red on the right—hold up a third section which is horizontal and filled with energized calligraphy in lush pastel colors. Collaged into the third section is an image of a rooster—the mirror image of the collaged rooster in the lower right-hand corner. One wants to allude to rebirth and death here, but Hudson dissuades, saying, "I probably just liked the look of those things as much as anything."

In another work on paper, Untitled, 1977 (cat. 79), the space is again divided into two portions. A collaged figure, which looks as if he stepped directly out of Gray's famous anatomy book, walks from one section of the work to another, leaving behind him a bird of deep blue-black, which could be Edgar Allan Poe's raven. A swirl of rich orange pastel forms the ground on the left and supports a wooden fan of multicolored sticks. As he leaves the "frame" of the first half of the work, the collaged anatomical figure gestures toward a "space window," a gridded window into the beyond which Hudson often incorporates into his works. Here the "space window" is cut into a rainbowed nest of pastel calligraphic marks. In this work, the collage elements inform and add mystery to the content because they now cause the work to exist on some curious plane half-way between realism and abstraction.

Another work of the same genre, yet one with an entirely different sensibility, is *Portrait,* 1978 (p. 53). This work eschews the vibrant colors which are Hudson's trademark, and instead takes on a Goya-like severity of black and white. Here a portrait of a Spanish nobleman forms the central image. Torn from its original context, the work now rests firmly attached to its black-and-white surroundings on a kind of revolving screen which seems to reverse in and out visually like a necker cube, appearing and disappearing at will.[4] About the central image a frenzied network of marks both more strident and more baroque than usual fill the surface of the work. If this work is somewhat atypical, it is a strong one which gives full voice to Hudson's graphic sensibilities.

Returning to color and continuing his enigmatic use of collage, Hudson created Untitled, 1979 (p. 48), one of the finest works on paper in the exhibition, which includes virtually all of his trademarks. Overlapping planes, discontinued elipses, and folding screens of space are a foil for the artist's now familiar primary palette. Painting boldly in a riot of reds, yellows, and blues, Hudson draws, rolls, and sculpturally shapes space like a master, finishing it off with a large, poignant collage of a deer which he plays off against a much smaller collage of peas and onions—why we do not know—while below, the planet Earth revolves luminously in space.

Throughout Hudson's work, globes of the world, balls, and large orbs figure prominently in the pieces—the world globes for their "feel" and allover patterning and for their capacity to bring all of the implications of Earth to the work in a single symbol, and the orbs or balls because he likes the shape. There is a fascination, too, with the curve of the earth, and it appears again and again in his work. It is in the artist's repetition of symbols and images such as these that we understand the importance of specific symbols for Hudson, although in his inimitably taciturn manner he manages always to dissuade the viewer from seeing them as overtly content laden. It should be reinforced that it is the visual look and "feel," rather than the intellectual implications, which appeal to the artist, and to attempt to translate the symbols is to overintellectualize a body of work that takes its strength from intuition and sensation rather than ordered, rational processes.

One such work, Untitled, 1980 (p. 54), is a perfect case in point. Here a hatchet, with a confetti-covered handle, chops deeply into the implied space of the work—past a 1930s paper fan with a marcelled beauty smiling vacuously—and, moving beyond a scroll of abstract imagery, imbeds its tip in two vertical panels of black and white in the upper left corner. It would be tempting here to say that Hudson, in his own Bay Area fashion, is hacking away at the sacred dichotomy of deep versus shallow space (implied

by the 1930s beauty on the flat fan), but Hudson would view such an interpretation as pretentious and would simply laugh it off. Interpretations aside—the piece works—and that is all we care about.

Another work which seems to tackle sacred cows head on is Untitled, 1980 (p. 52). This is a Hudson classic. Here, amidst brilliant color exquisitely inset into a graphed and gridded framework, the artist cuts through the formalist ground and its flat, layered grid as if with an X-acto knife so that it "bleeds" a profusion of multicolored planets, globes, and confetti which roll and tumble out through great spatial depth toward the viewer. The depth and momentum of this imagery is further underscored by the demure image of a 1920s fashion plate with a fan, while in the lower right-hand corner a woman with a bowling ball aims directly for the viewer. Again, it is tempting to see this work as historically "important" because of its tongue-in-cheek historical implications—yet that would be to miss the point. The issue perhaps is that the point can be made visually—and that is an important one, for with Hudson we are always dealing with art—and not with art history.

Throughout the body of Hudson's works there are also totally abstract works as well, works which give themselves over to the sheer visual pleasure of imagery on paper. It is perhaps in these works that the viewer can take full pleasure in the sensuousity of the work itself—because there is no literal image to decode or to translate. Untitled, 1974 (cat. 75), is an interesting case in point. In this work the space is divided into two, like the pages of a book. The images are architectonic: curious structures that seem to exist in space, providing room for the forms which inhabit them. Rectangular, flat, or scrolled, the overlapping planes that fill the space take shape through the medium of wiry energized charcoal lines which seem almost to draw themselves in a frenzy of automatic writing. Glowing intensely, the hot pastels burn up the paper from within, like embers stoked alive from ashes. The balance here is so impeccable, the shaping so secure, that there is real pleasure in the innate sense of order as well as in the power of the color.

Another totally abstract work is Untitled, 1979 (p. 52). This drawing is a Copernican fantasy—a cosmological chart created by a mad astrologer in which worlds whirl and collide, connected by powerful force lines and spattered with nebular confetti. Peculiarly, maddeningly erratic, Hudson has defined the largest planet in this delirious universe by the image of a large paper lace doily sprinkled with white paint as if frosted with powdered sugar.

The most tactile of the abstract works on paper is Untitled, 1982 (cat. 101). Made of cast, handmade paper, this work has delicate squares of lace which float through the brushy ground on both sides of the work. A stick

4. Necker cube: an ambiguous figure. A situation is set up in which the eye is given two sets of perspectives and is unable to make a choice between the two.

figure with an elegant lace head occupies one side of
the composition. Above it all is a fragment of a shaped,
architectonic detail painted red, yellow, and blue which
is affixed to the top of the work like the body parts
at the top of Jasper Johns's well-known *Target*.

Robert Hudson has been producing mature
works for more than twenty-five years. He first came to
prominence when he was still in graduate school at the
San Francisco Art Institute. During that theoretically
unformed period in his life, he was producing remarkably
sophisticated polychromed sculptures.

Hudson has always made his own rules. He overpainted his early trompe l'oeil sculpture, ignoring, changing,
denying their three-dimensional sculptural quality. Con-
versely, the new paintings and works on paper appear
deeply three-dimensional and profoundly sculptural. Where
Hudson once made sculpture go flat, he now makes paintings
that feel as if they are being viewed in the round. Yet today,
with an even greater degree of sophistication and perver-
sity, he continues to tap the same rich, visual reservoir
which provided the images for his sculptures. His works are
so good that they make us realize suddenly why it is okay
to paint again. In the hands of such an artist, painting has
found the kind of voice that has been lost for decades.

Private Lenders

Deborah Allen, Medford, New Jersey
Stephen S. Alpert Family Trust
Wayne Andersen, Boston
Mr. and Mrs. Harry W. Anderson, Atherton, California
Robert Arneson and Sandra Shannonhouse, Benicia, California
Adam Aronson, St. Louis
Matthew D. and Wanda Ashe, Sausalito, California
Atlantic Richfield Company Corporate Art Collection, Los Angeles
Patrick Brennan, San Francisco
Dr. and Mrs. Gerald Bush, Concord, Massachusetts
Wayne E. Campbell and Richard S. Canter, New York
The Capital Group, Inc., Los Angeles
James Cottrell, New York
Rene and Veronica de Rosa, Napa, California
Don and Nancy Eiler, Madison, Wisconsin
Dr. and Mrs. William R. Fielder, Atherton, California
Diana Fuller, San Francisco
Dorothy A. Goldeen, San Francisco
Wally Goodman, San Francisco
Robert Gordy, New Orleans
Alice and Martin Grossman, M.D., Miami Beach
Mr. and Mrs. Graham Gund
Hamilton-Wells Collection, San Francisco
Robert Hudson and Mavis Jukes, Cotati, California
Daniel Jacobs, New York
Mr. and Mrs. John Lowell Jones
Dr. and Mrs. Harold Joseph, St. Louis
Naomi and Robert Lauter, San Francisco
Sally Lilienthal, San Francisco
Byron Meyer, San Francisco
Mrs. Ralph J. Mills, Jr., Chicago
Mr. and Mrs. Edmund Nash, Belvedere, California
Manuel and Kate Neri, Benicia, California
Jerome and Margaret Nerman, Kansas City, Missouri
John and Mary Pappajohn, Des Moines
Jim Proby, San Francisco
The Prudential Insurance Company of America, Newark, New Jersey
Mr. and Mrs. C. David Robinson, Sausalito, California
Jane and Ruth Root
Audrey Sabol, Key Largo, Florida
Richard and Martha Shaw, Fairfax, California
Mr. and Mrs. Marvin Singer, Atlanta
Martin Sklar, New York
Jack and Rena Thompson, Chalfont, Pennsylvania
Laila and Thurston Twigg-Smith, Honolulu
Peter Voulkos, Oakland
Wellington Management/Thorndike, Doran, Paine & Lewis, Boston
Nicholas Wilder, New York
William T. Wiley, California
Mr. and Mrs. William Wilson III, Hillsborough, California
Laura-Lee Woods, Los Angeles
W. Scott Woods, San Francisco
Wright/Bonfilio, San Francisco

Institutions and Galleries

The Art Institute of Chicago
Central Iowa Art Association, Marshalltown
Allan Frumkin Gallery, New York
Frumkin & Struve Gallery, Chicago
Fuller Goldeen Gallery, San Francisco
Museum of Fine Arts, Boston
The Museum of Modern Art, New York
Philadelphia Museum of Art
San Francisco Museum of Modern Art
Stedelijk Museum, Amsterdam
University Art Museum, University of California, Berkeley

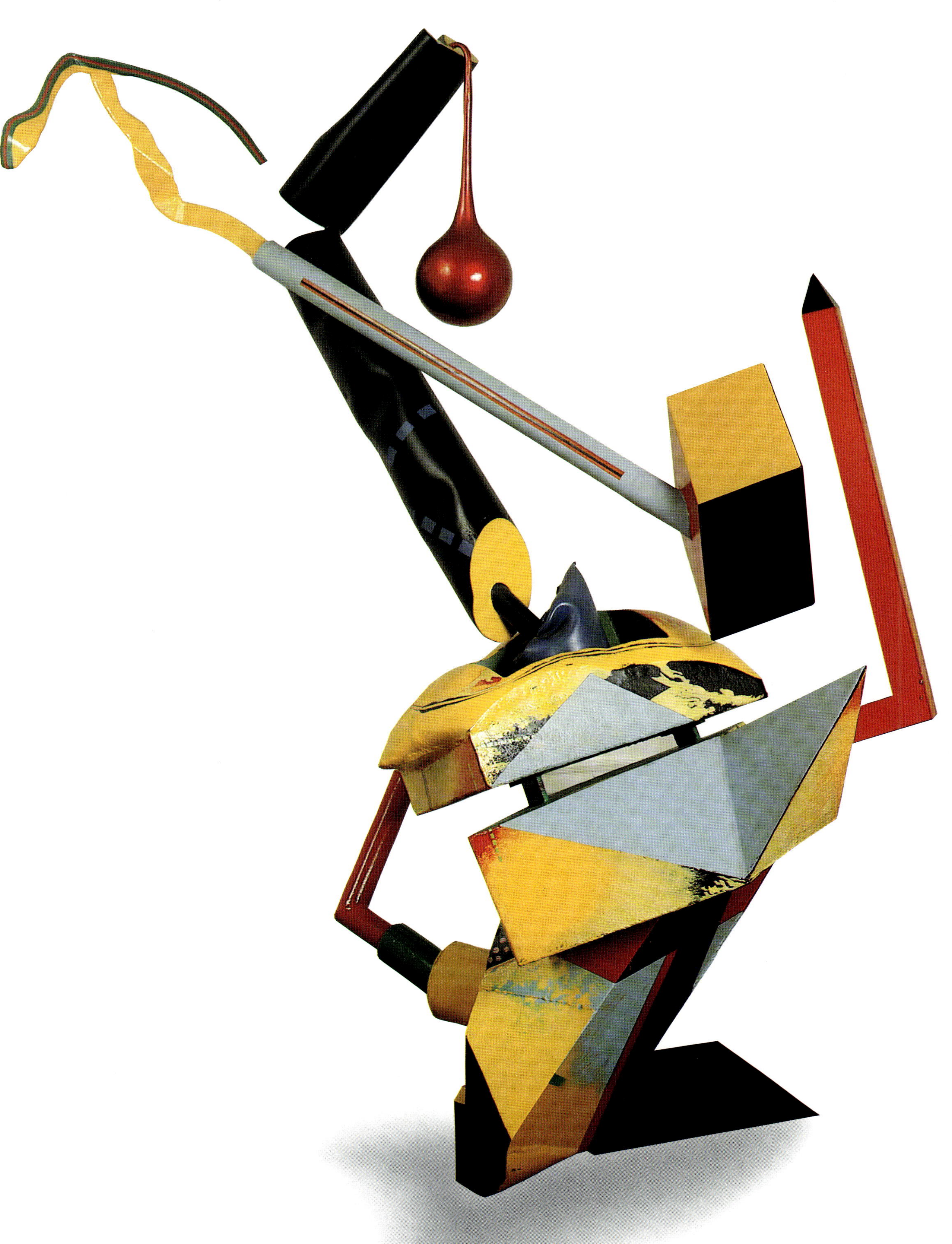

15. *Twisted Hip*, 1967

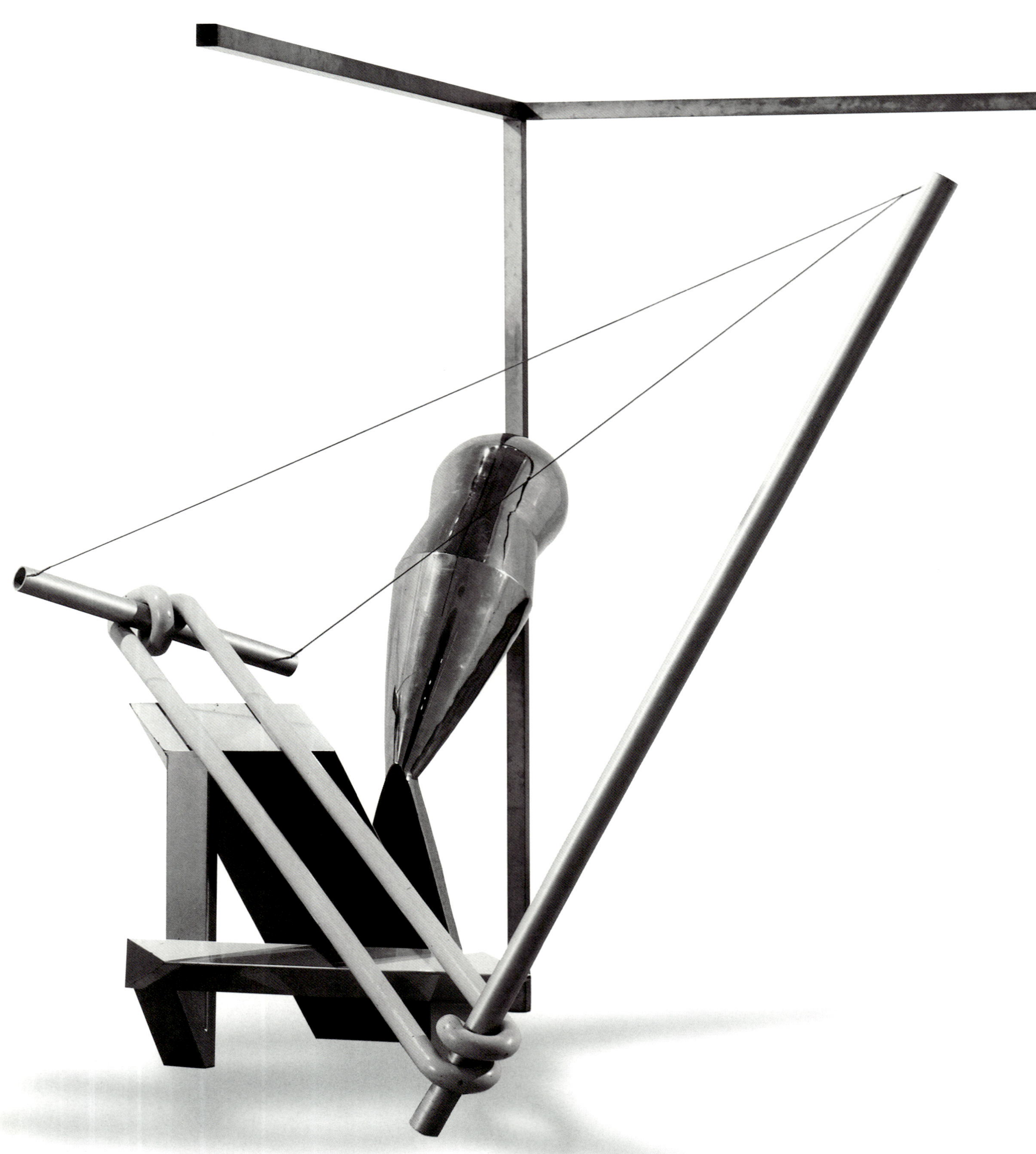

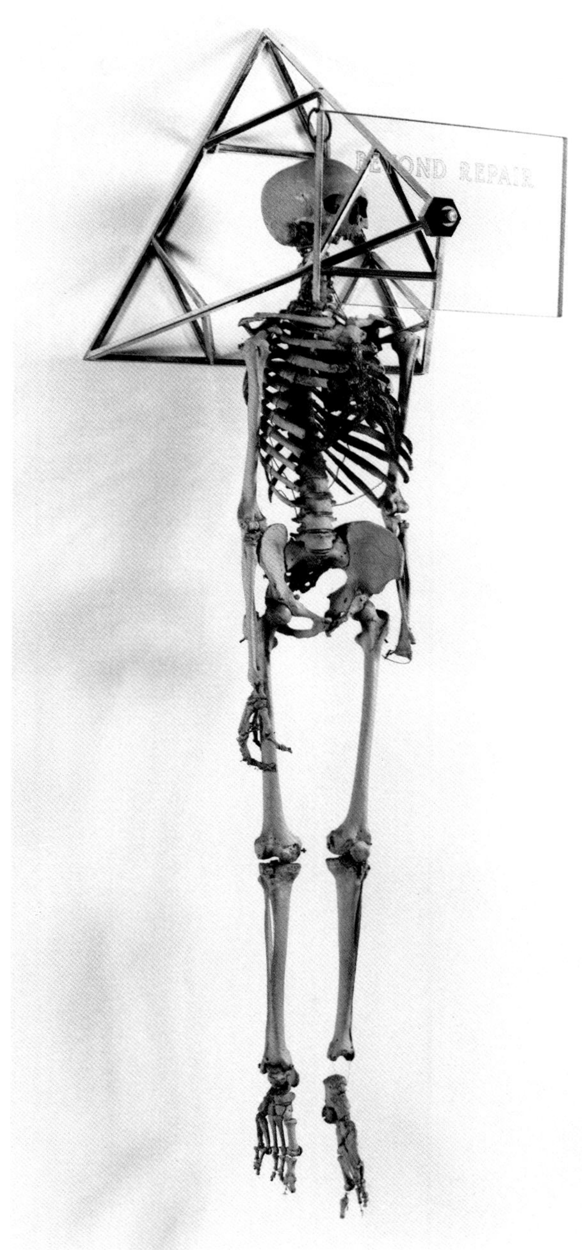
BEYOND REPAIR

Space Window, 1966

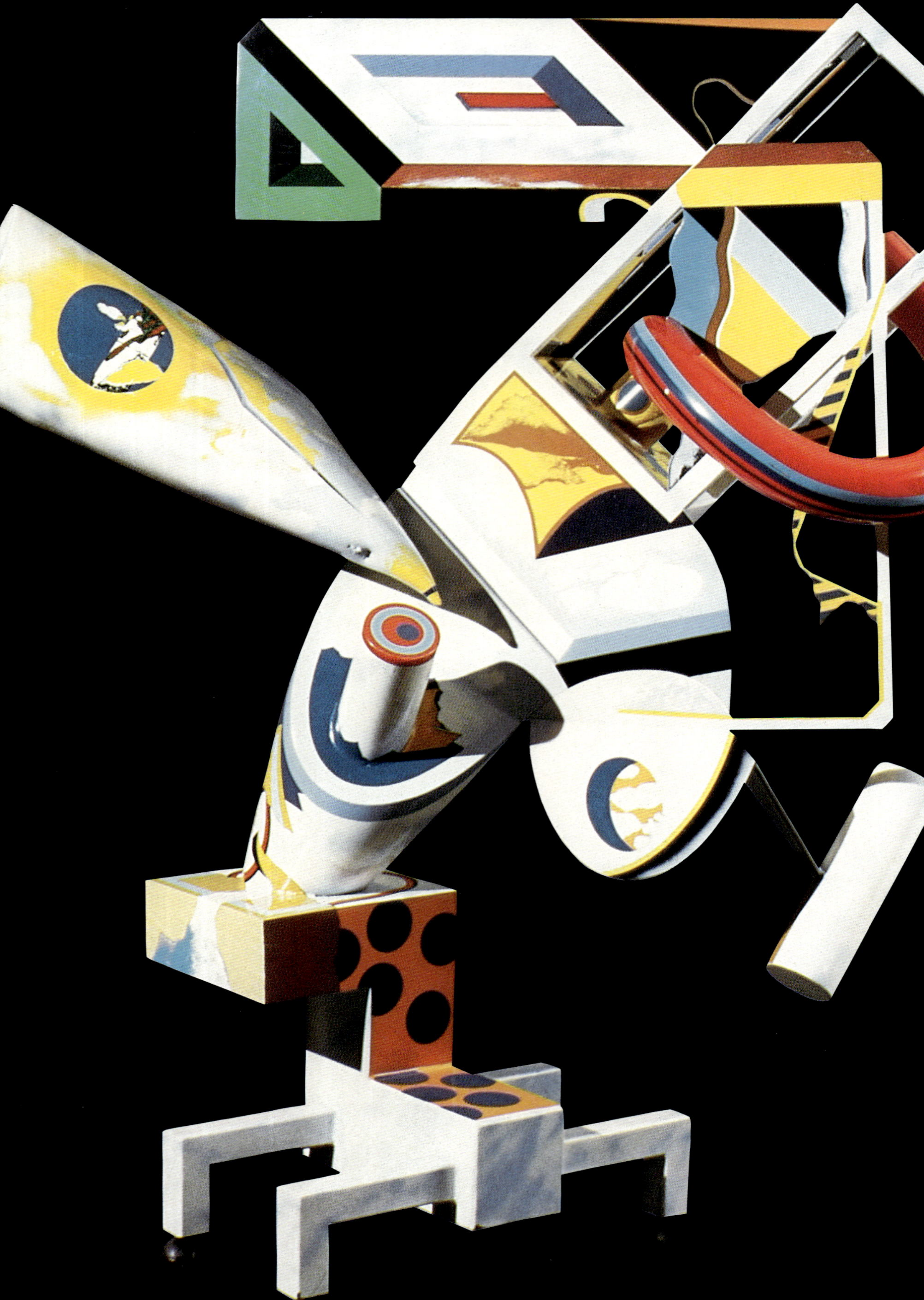

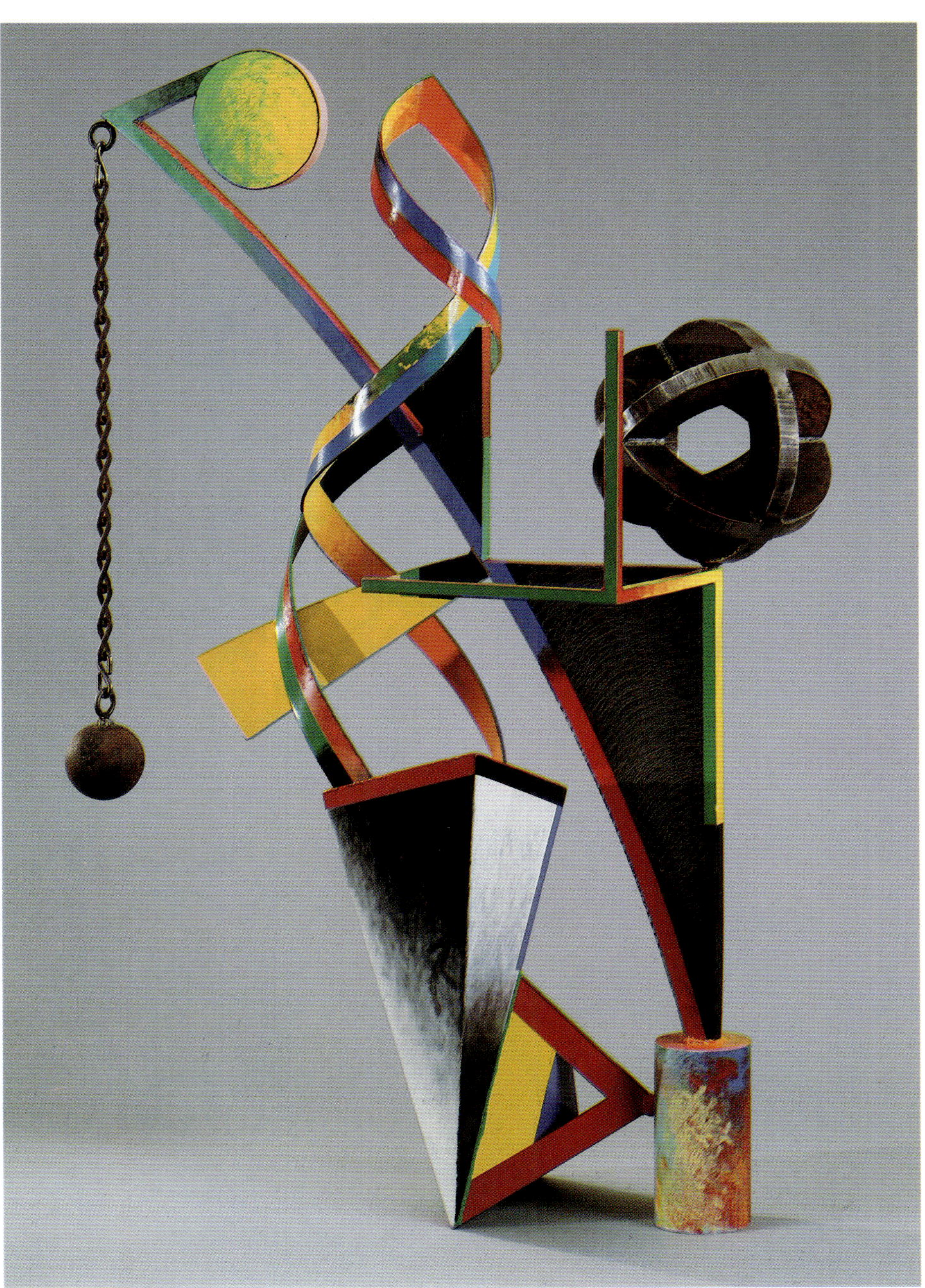

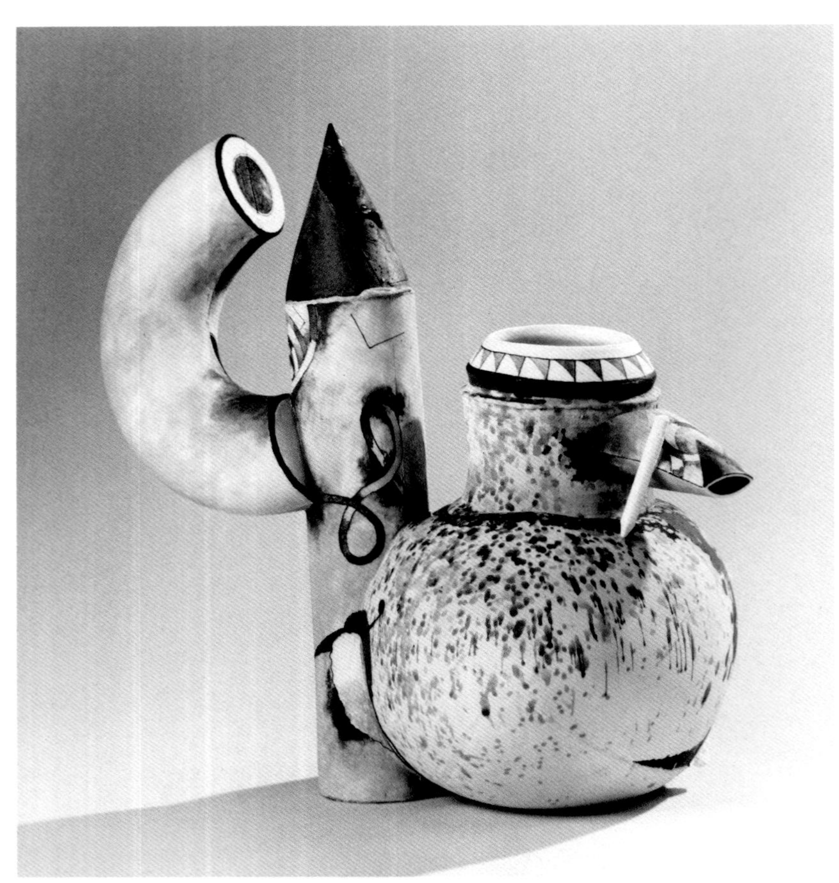

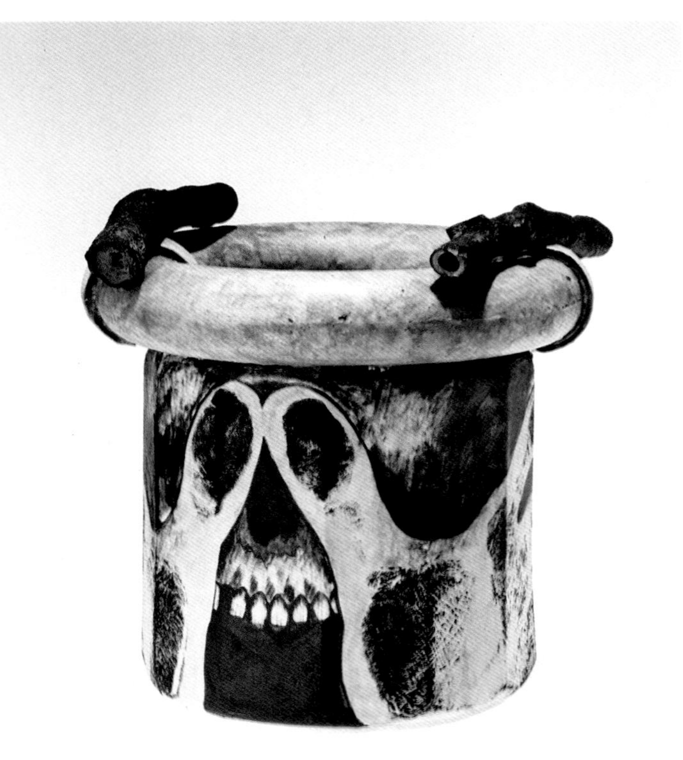

104. *Jar*, 1972

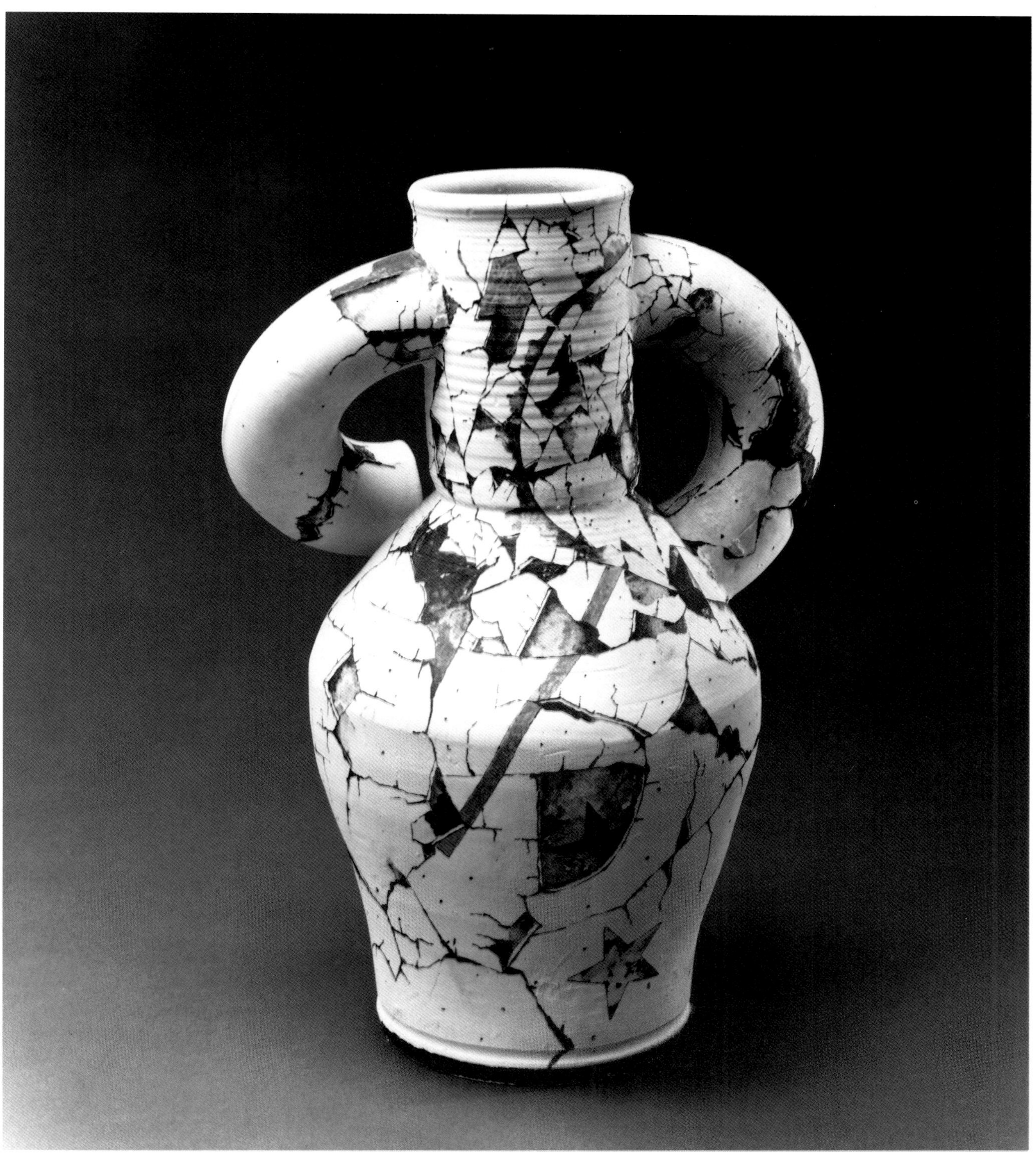

112. *Bowl*, 1973

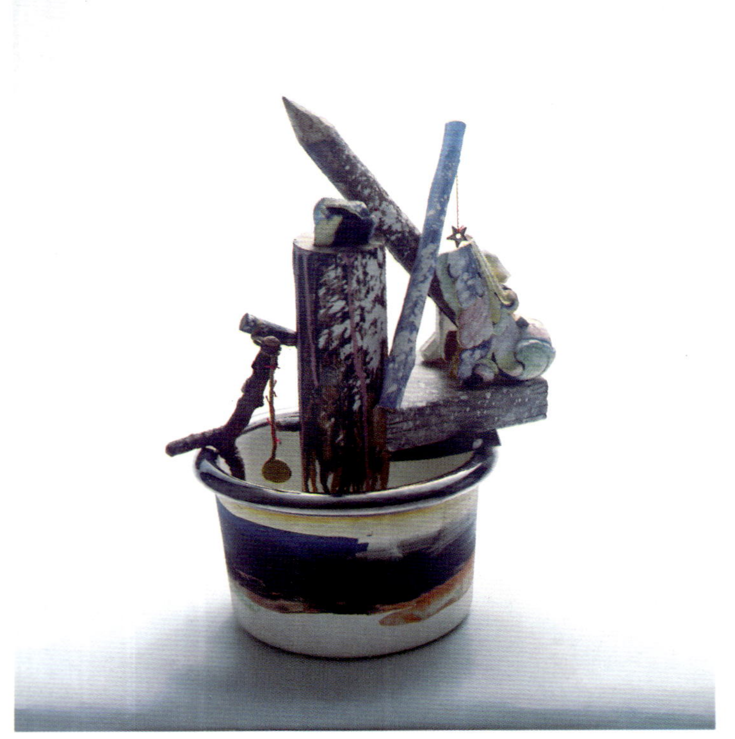

103. *Cup*, 1972

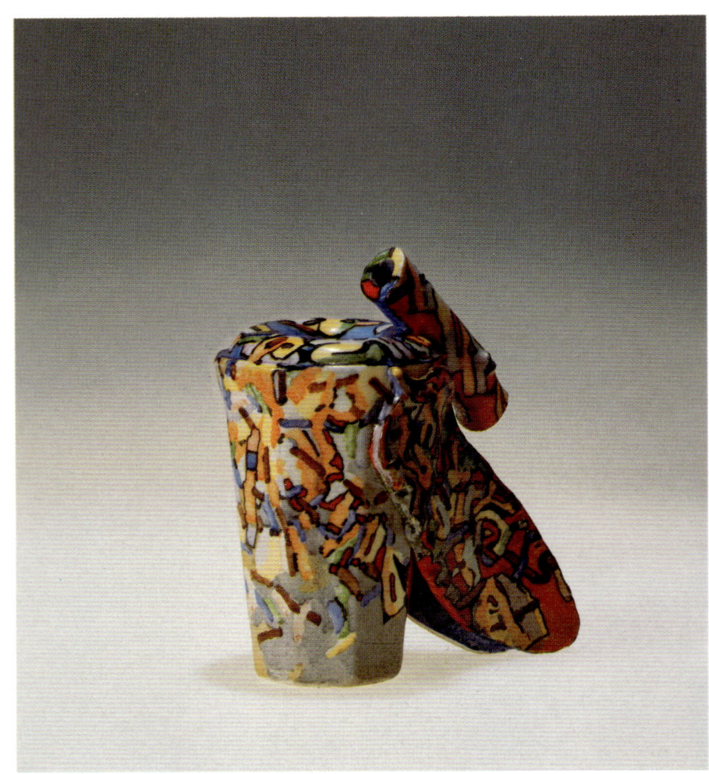

107. *Jar*, 1972-73

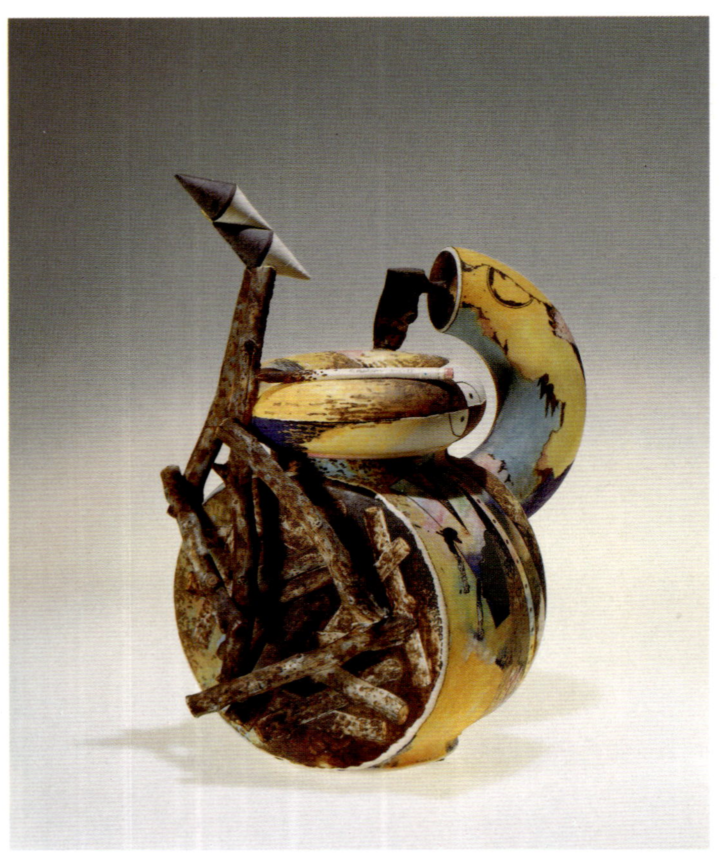

114. *Indian Pot*, 1973

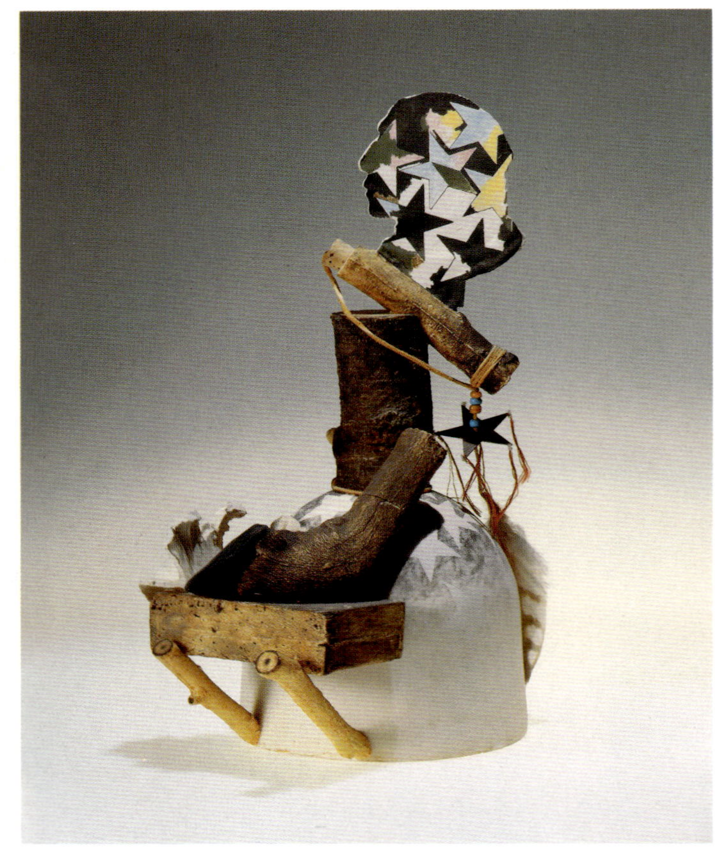

52. Untitled III, 1973

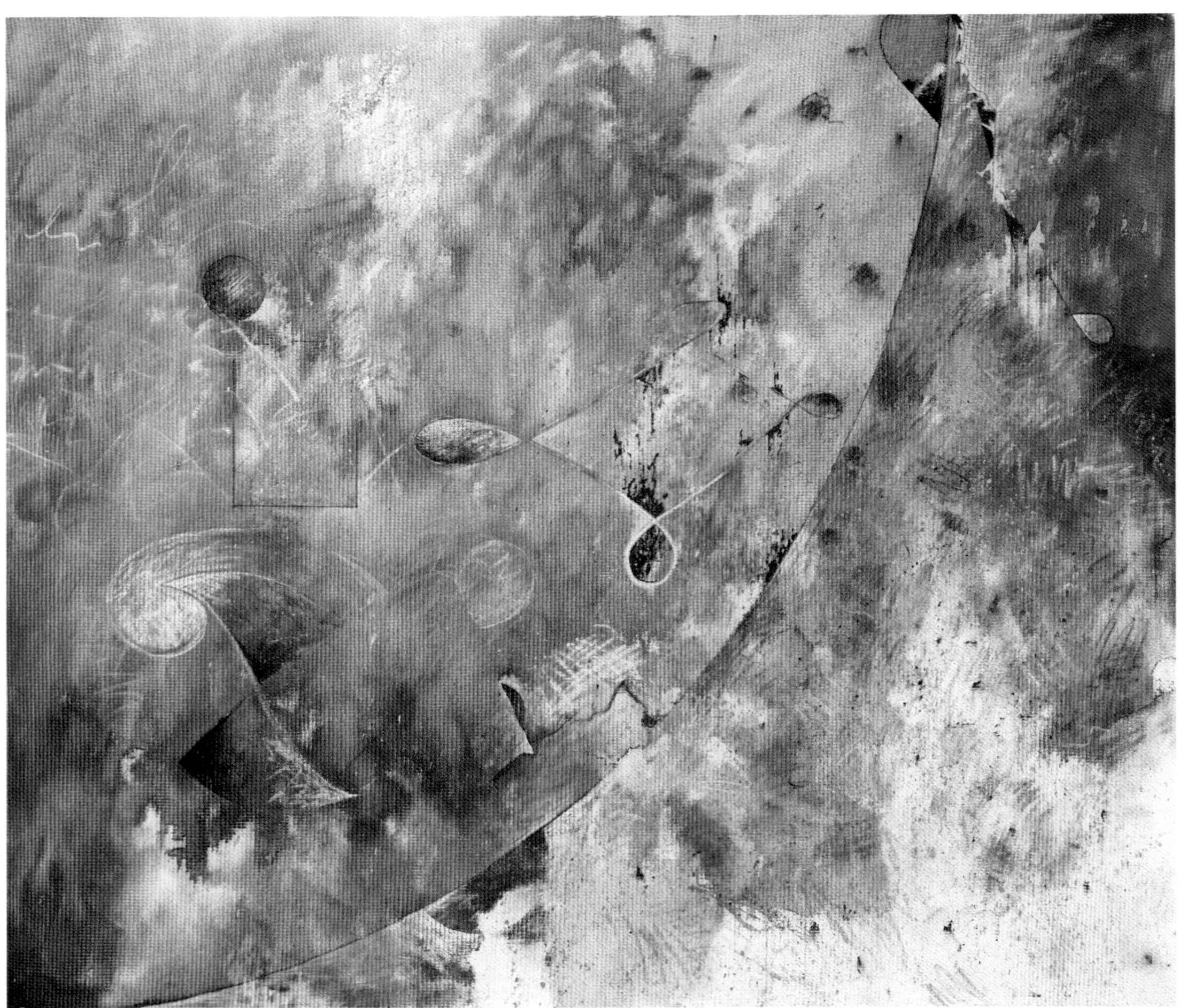

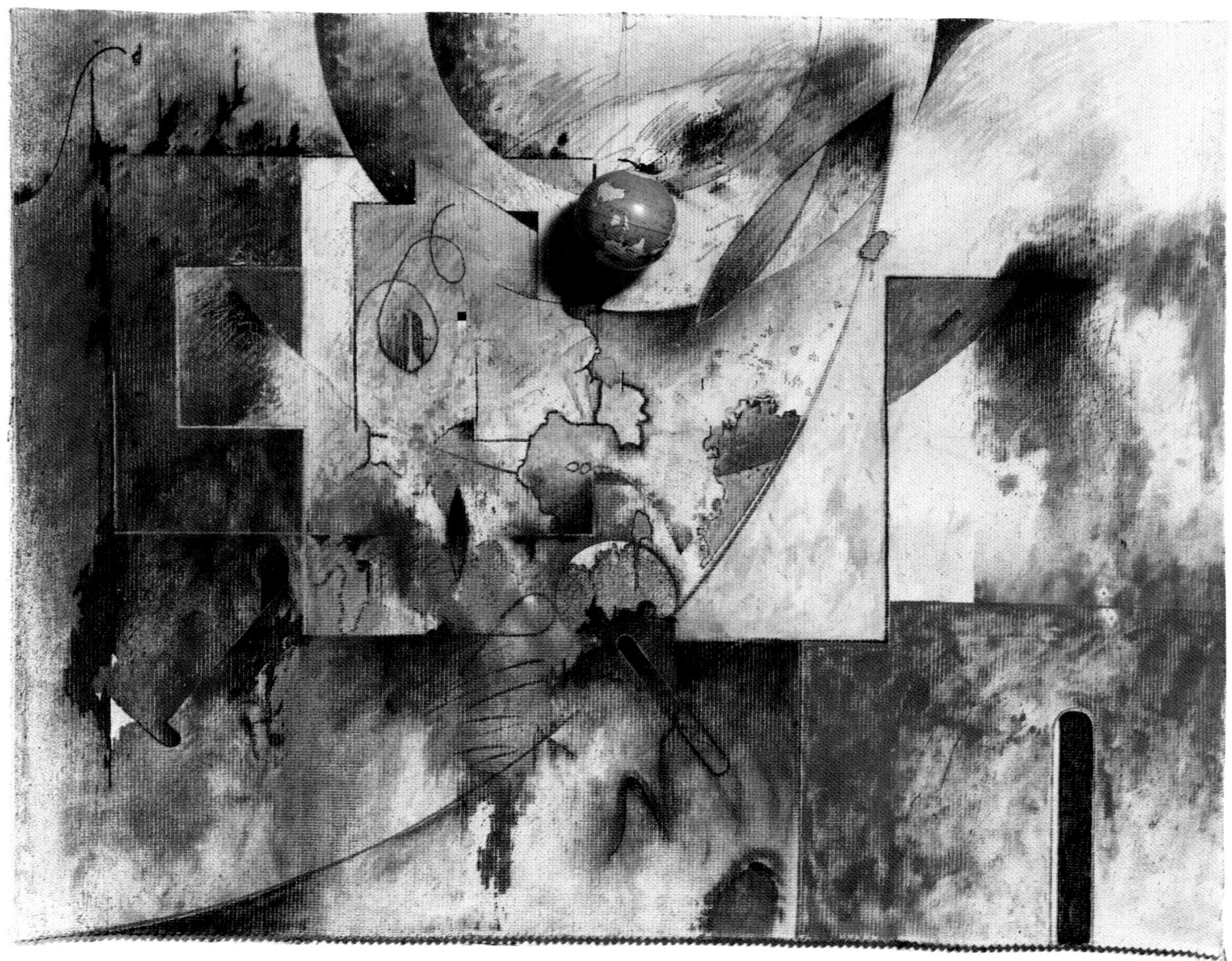

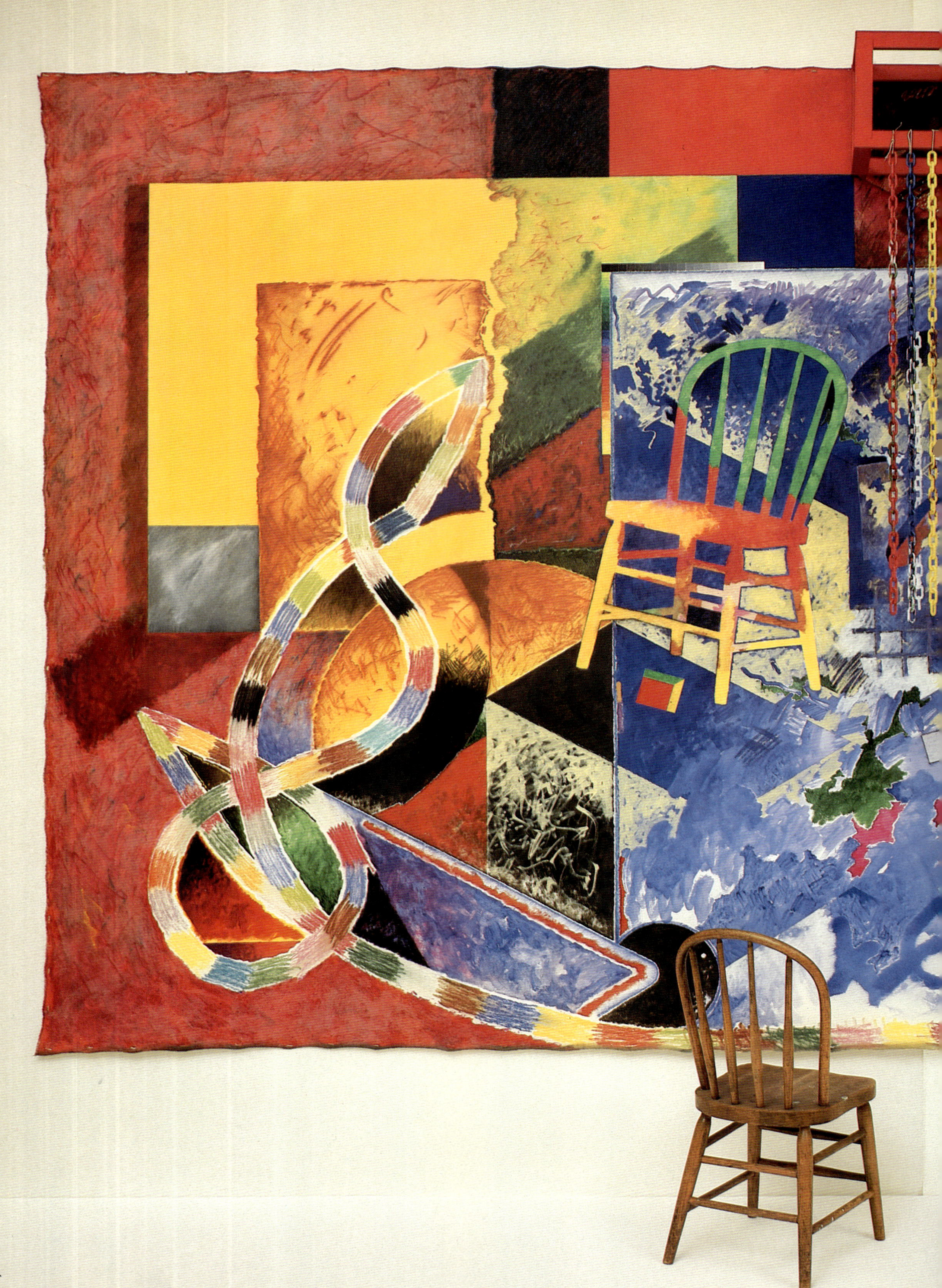

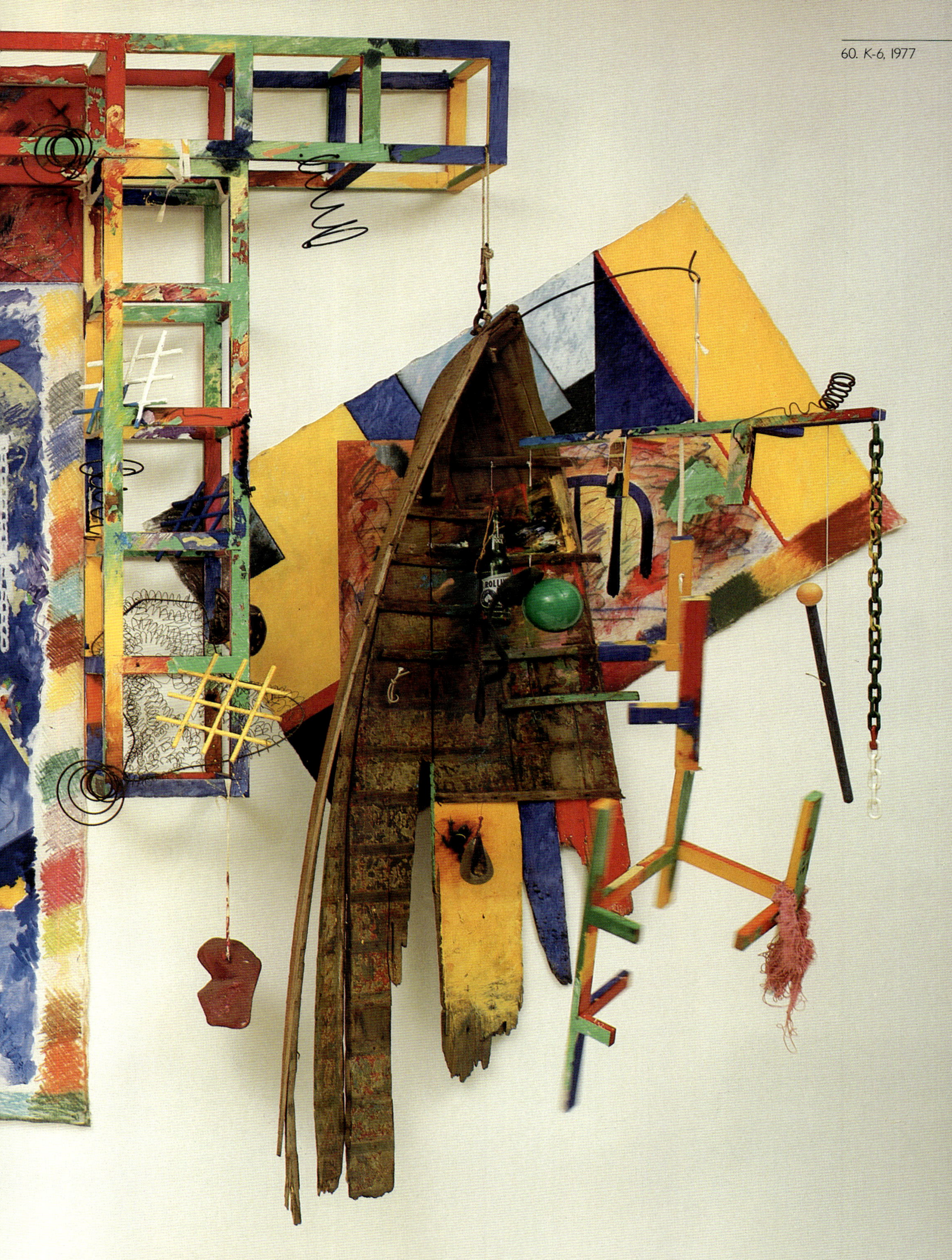

60. K-6, 1977

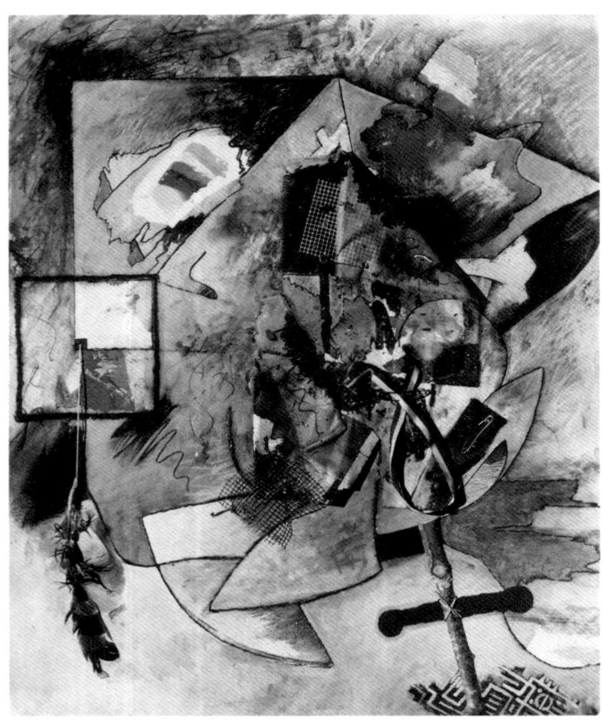

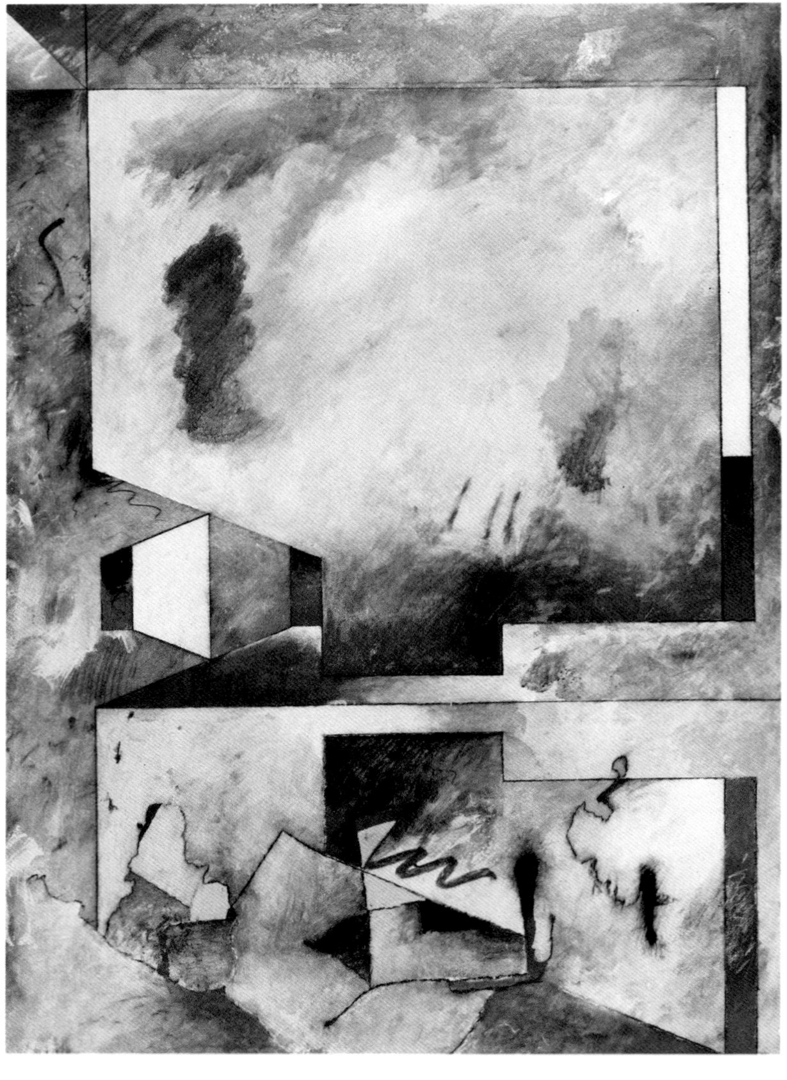

55. *Bear Claw*, 1976

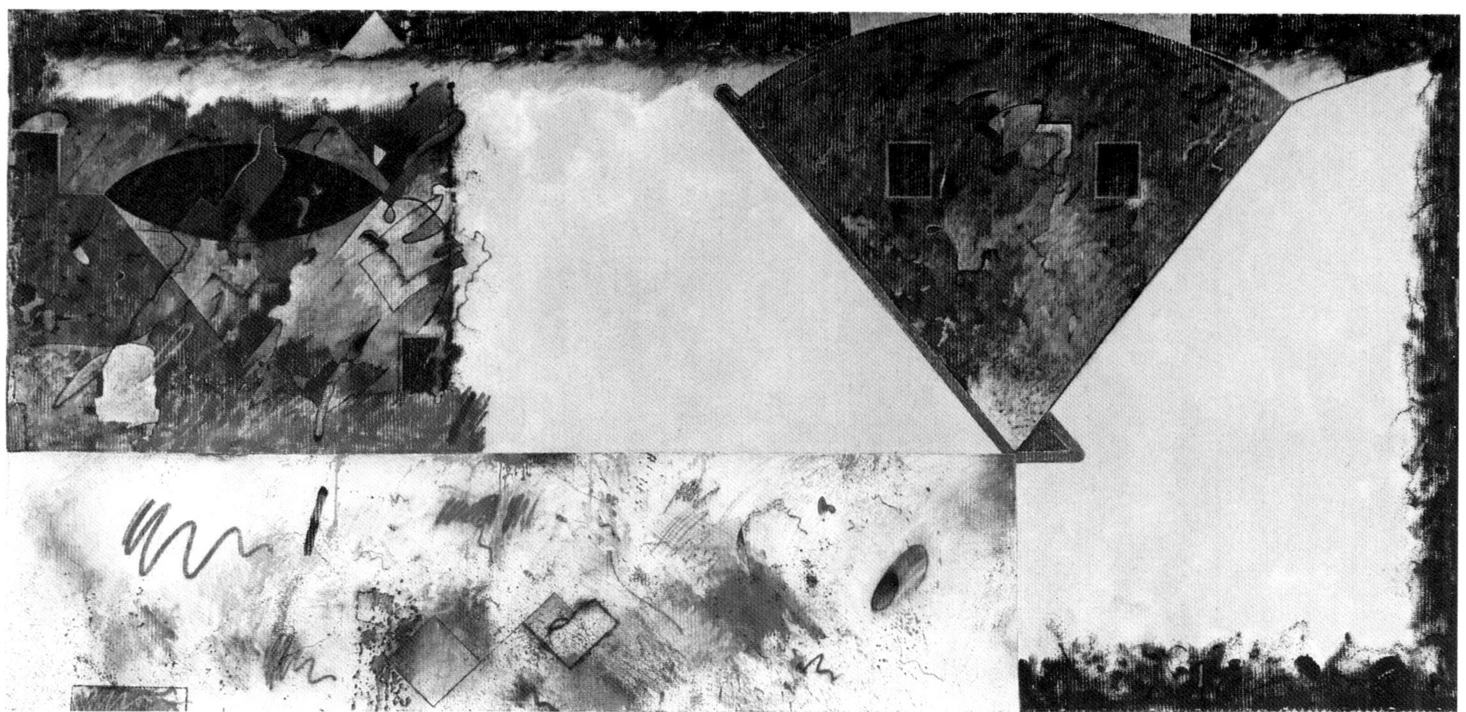

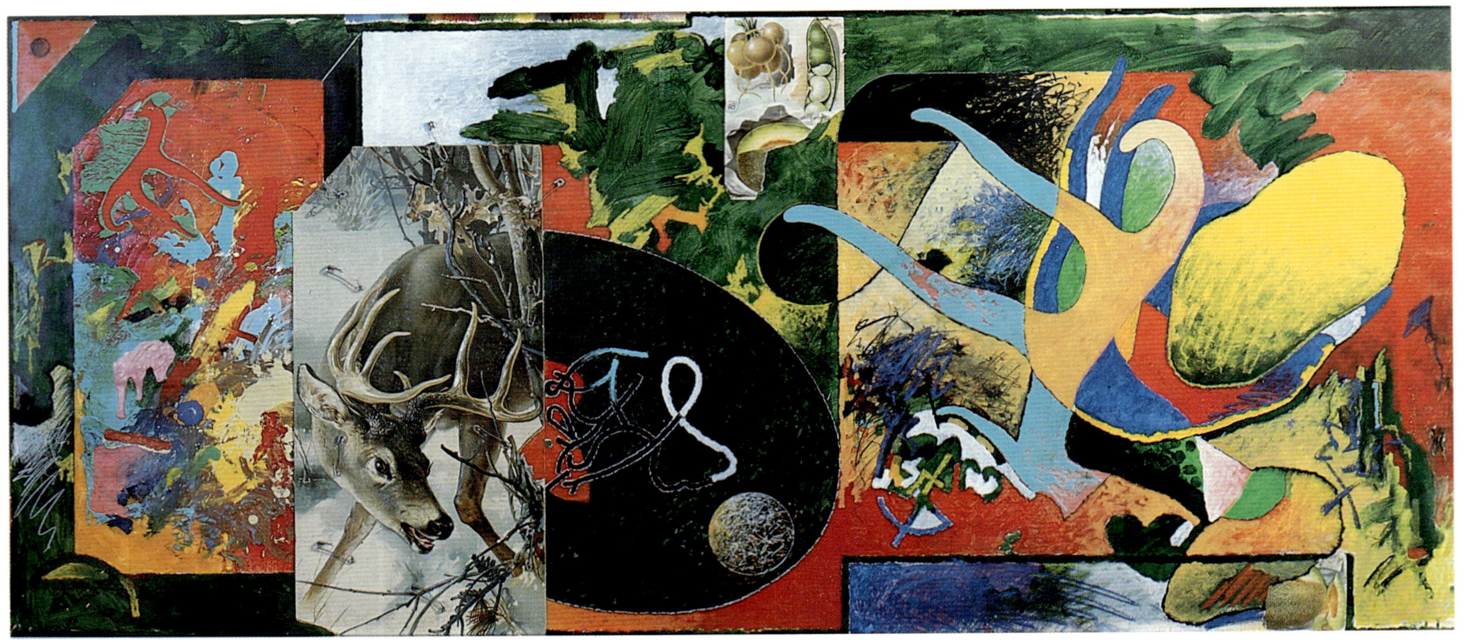

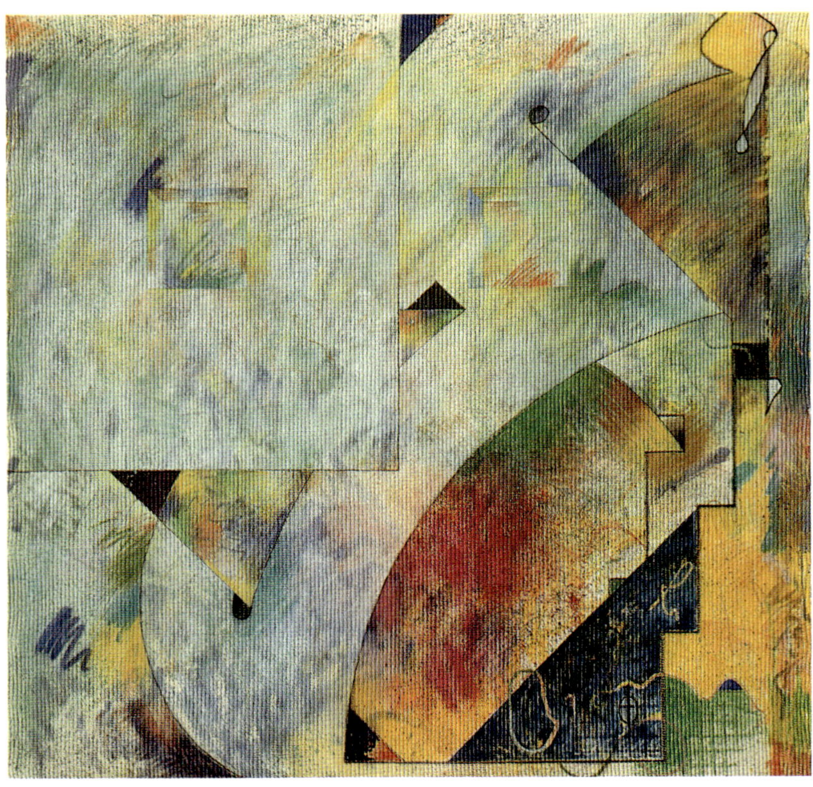

56. *Indian Woman*, 1976

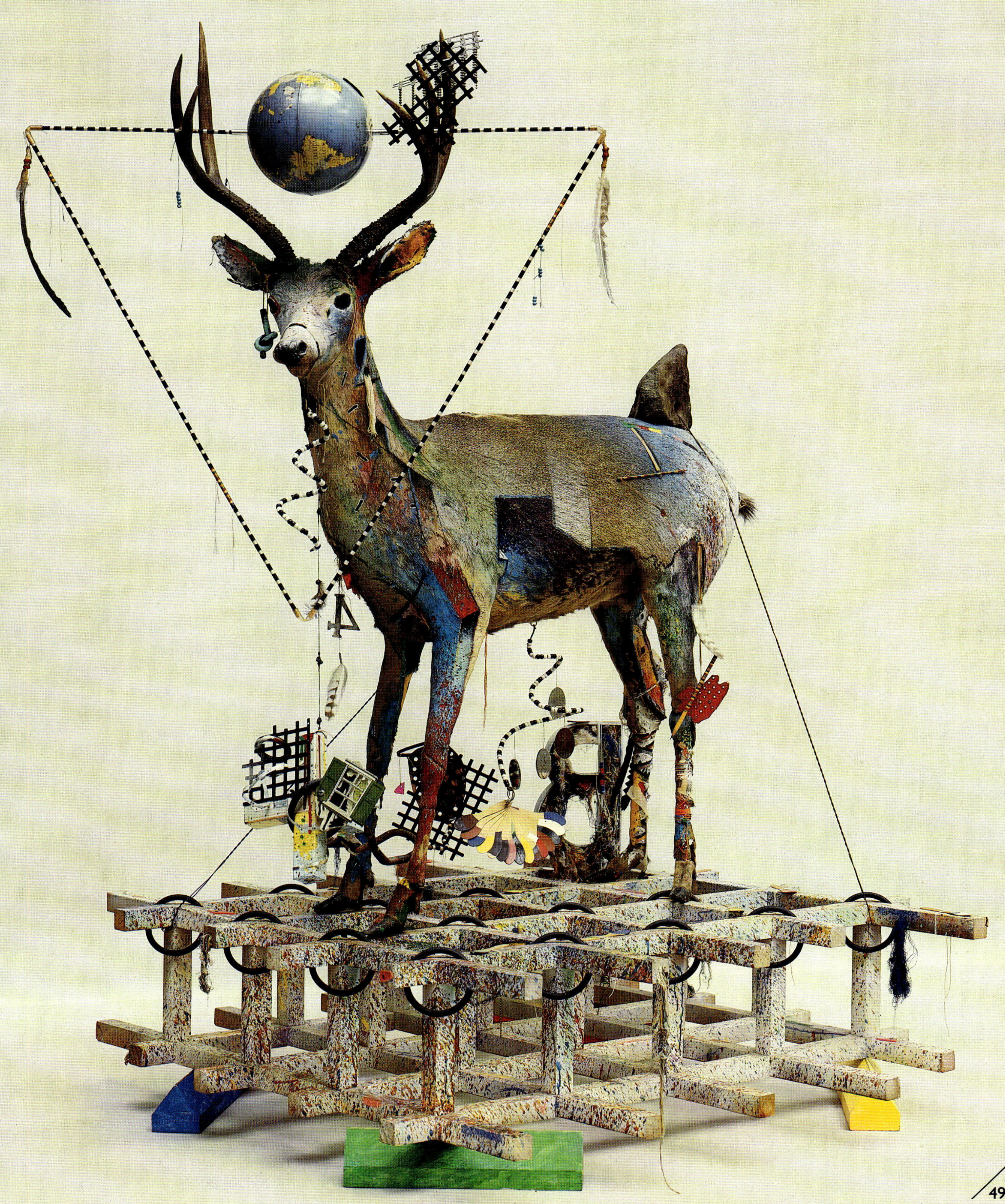

92. Untitled, 1979

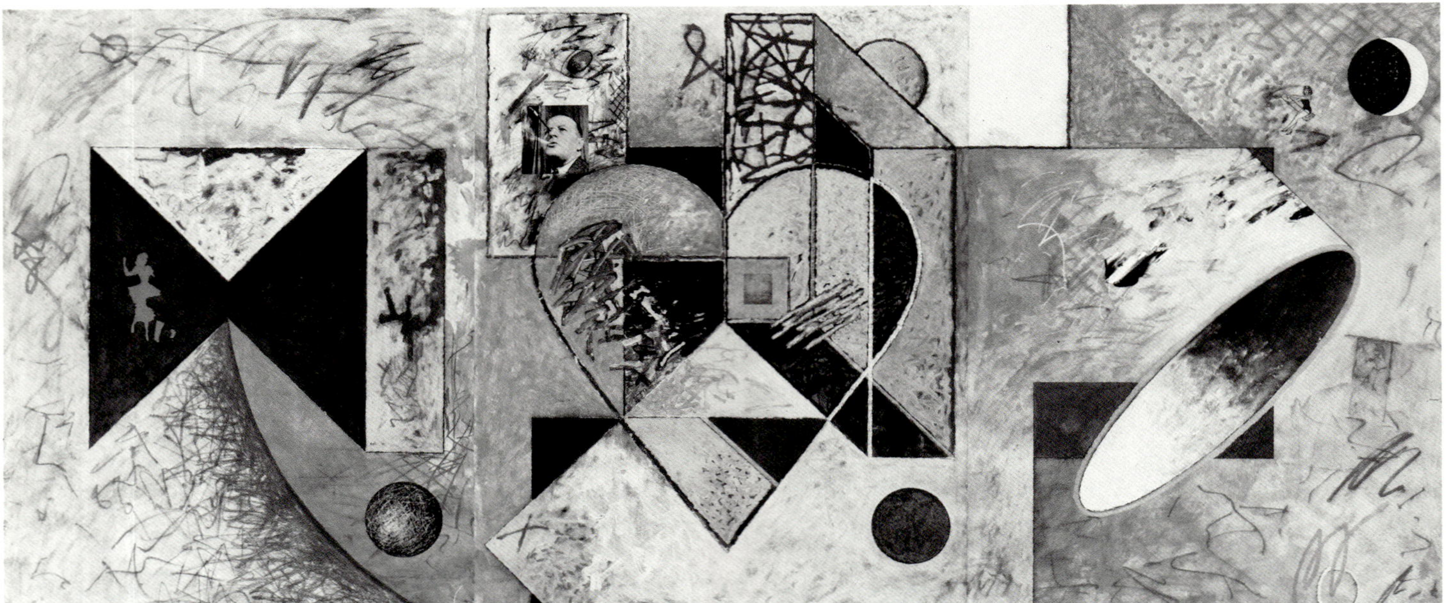

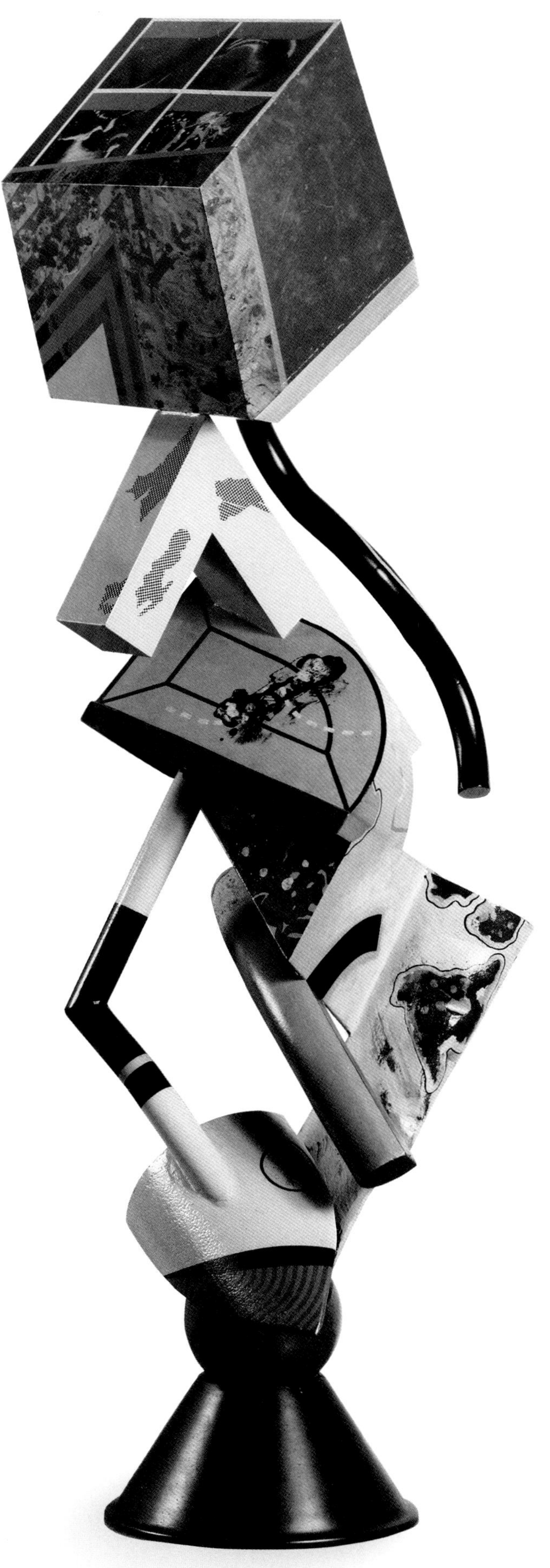

91. Untitled, 1979

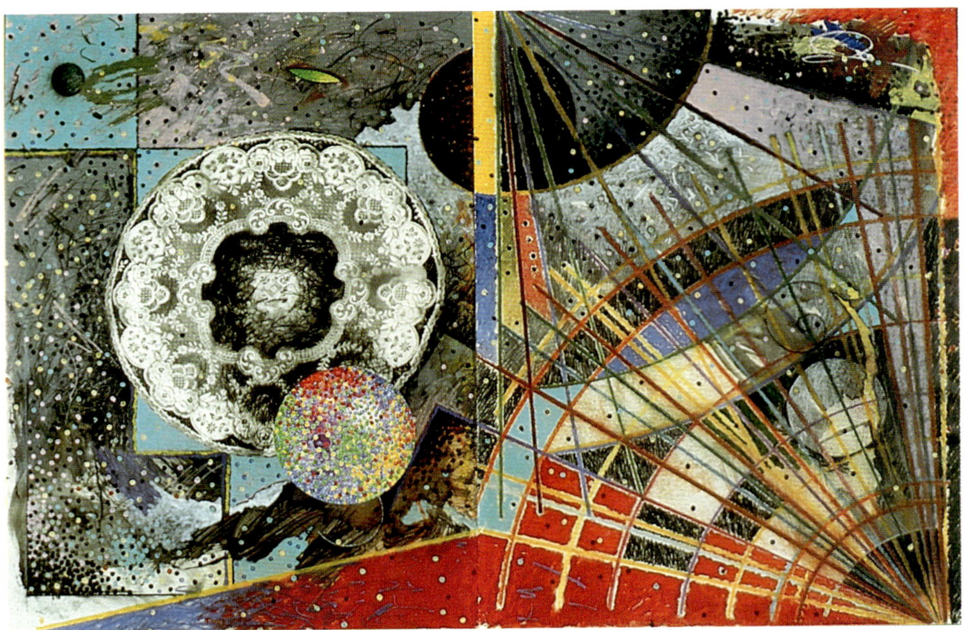

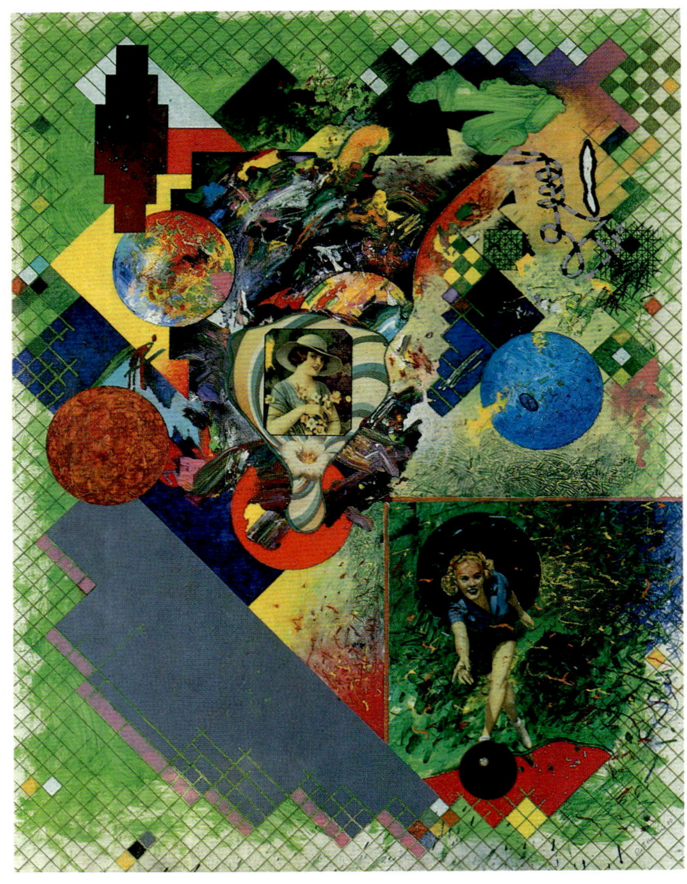

94. Untitled, 1980

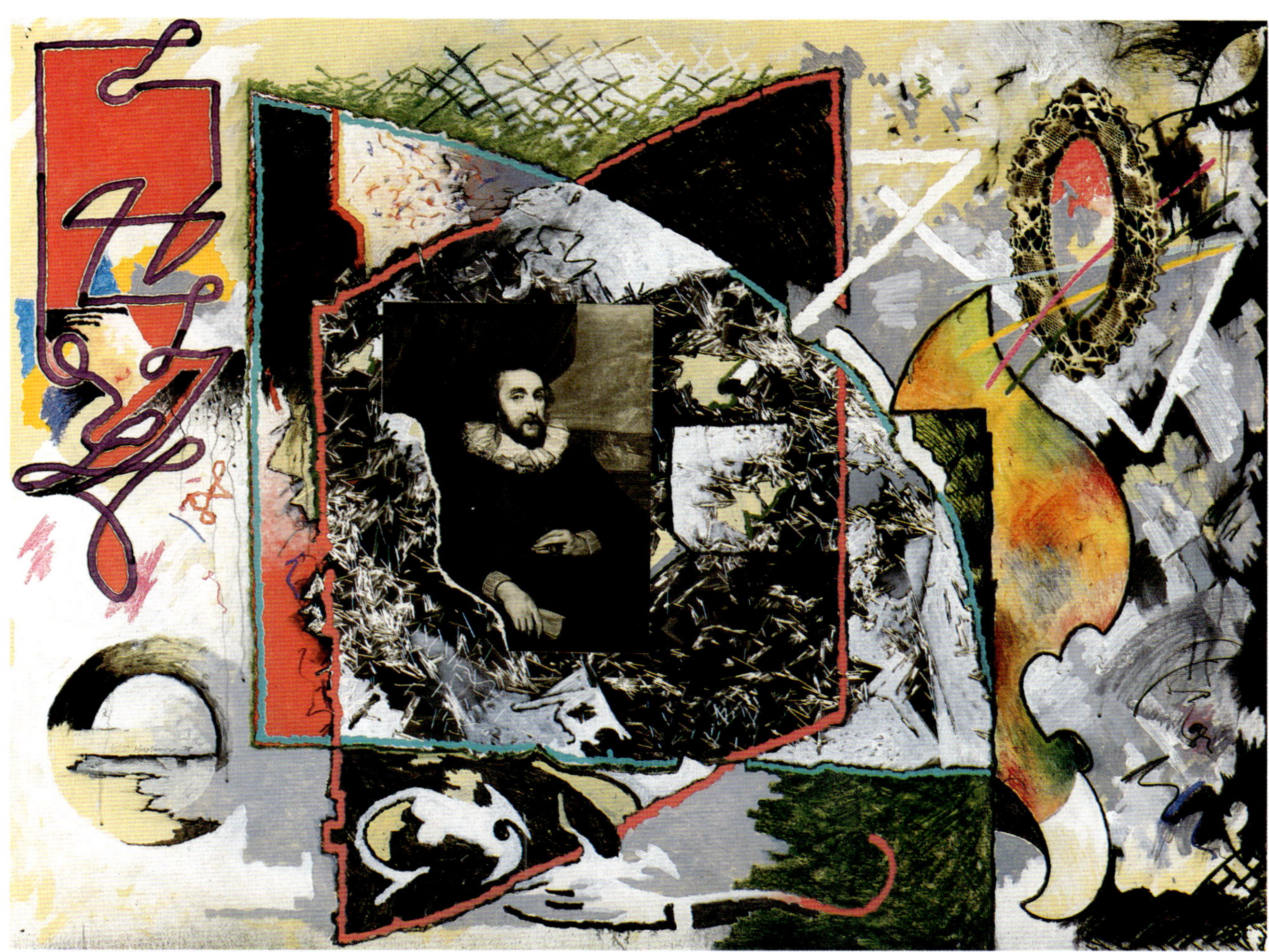

88. *Look*, 1979

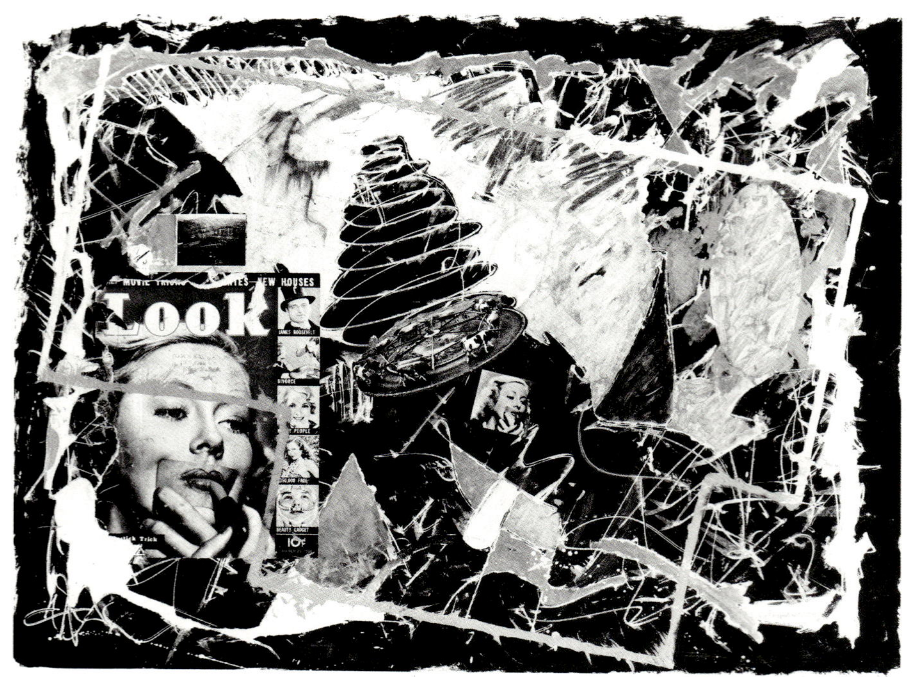

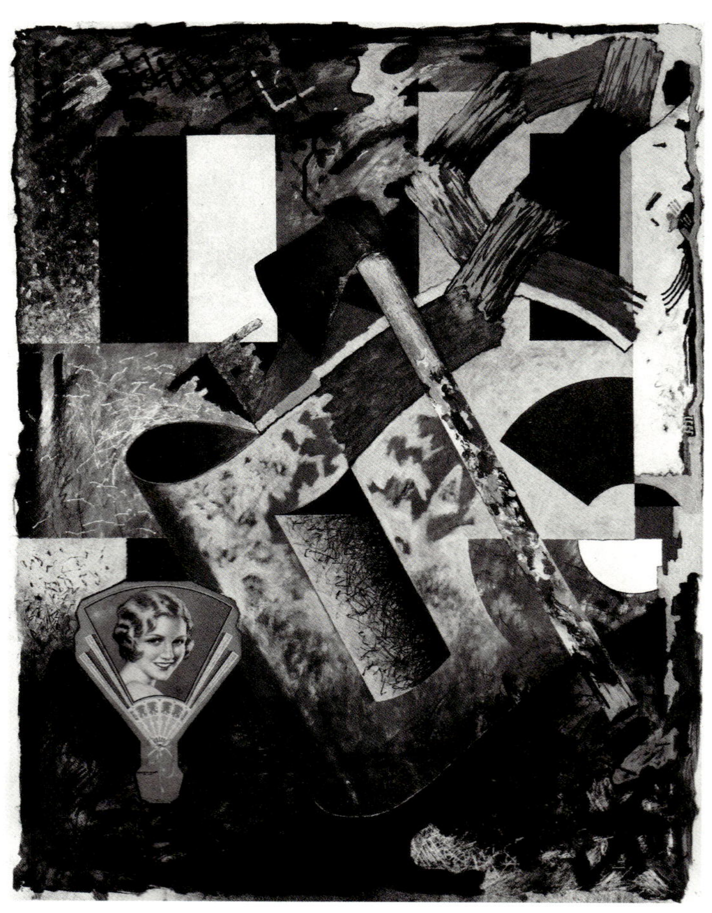

98. Untitled, 1980

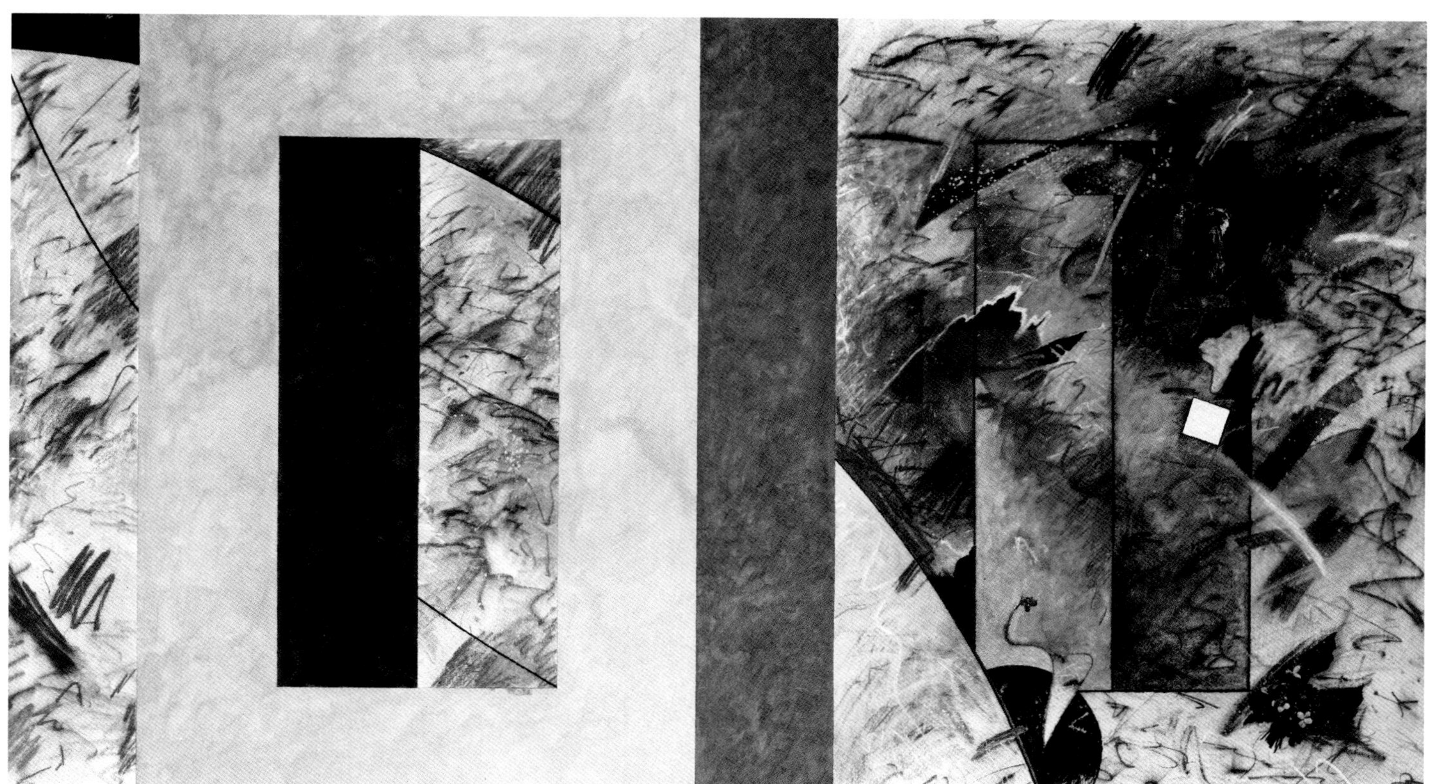

69. Untitled, 1980-81

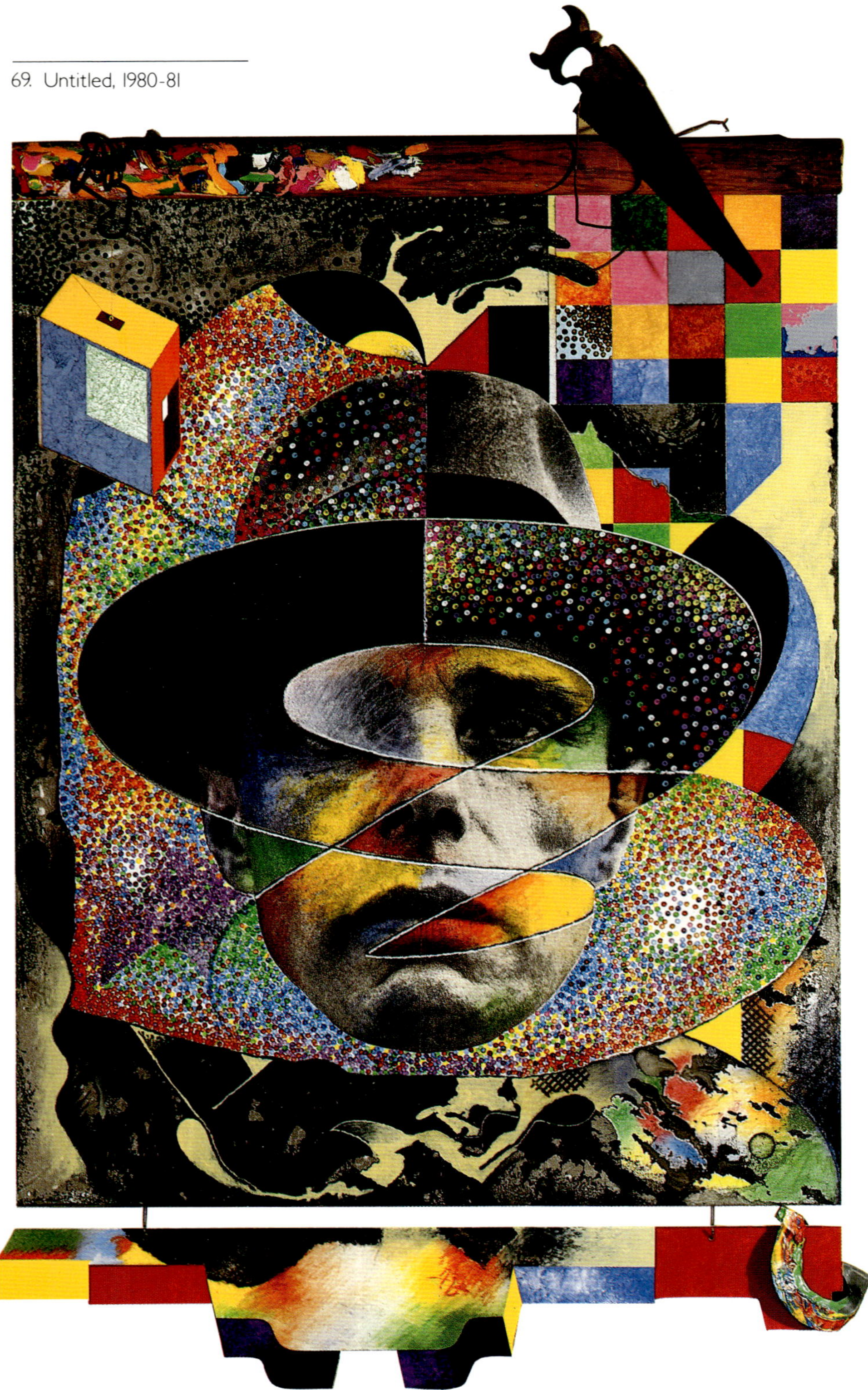

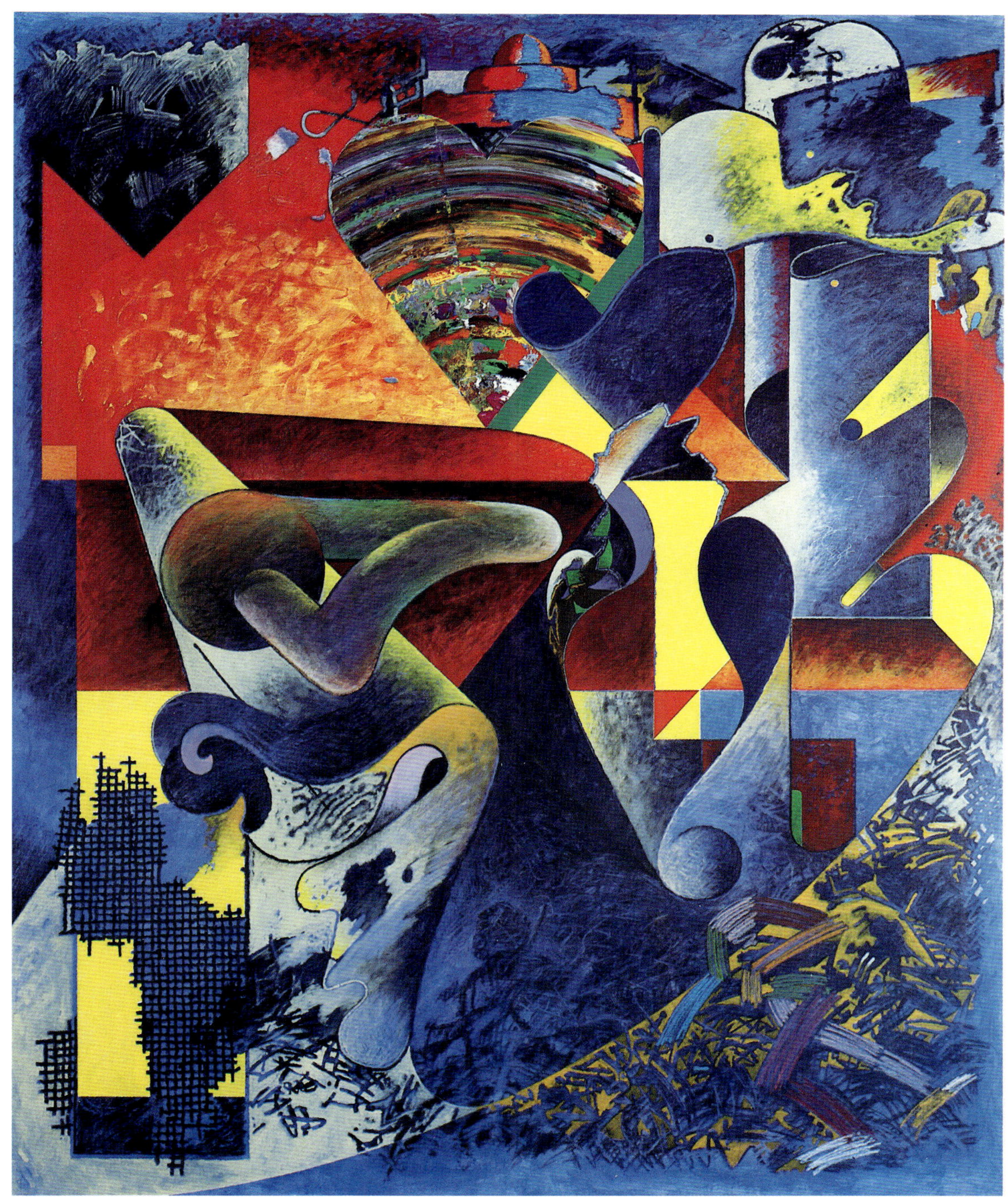

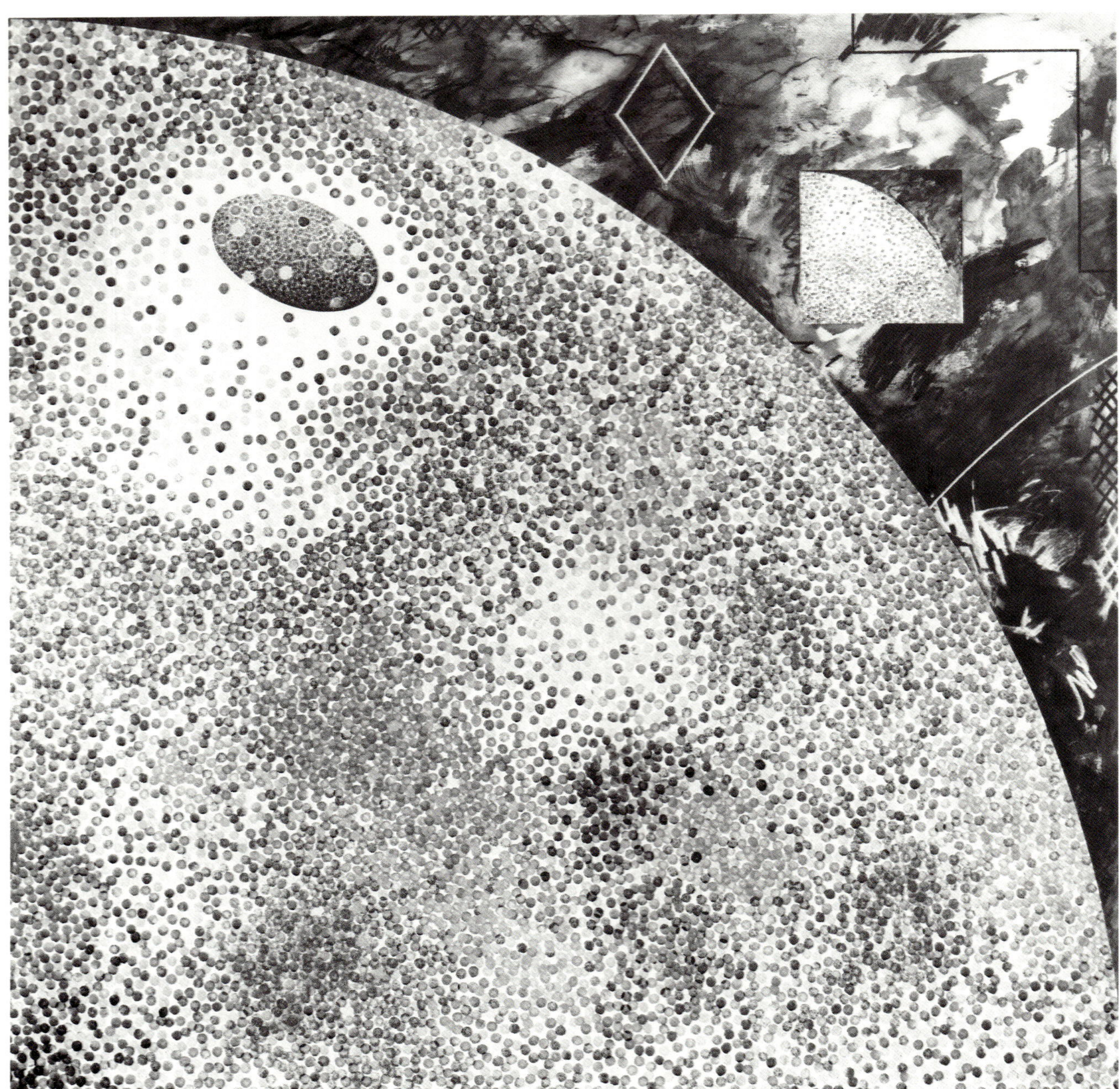

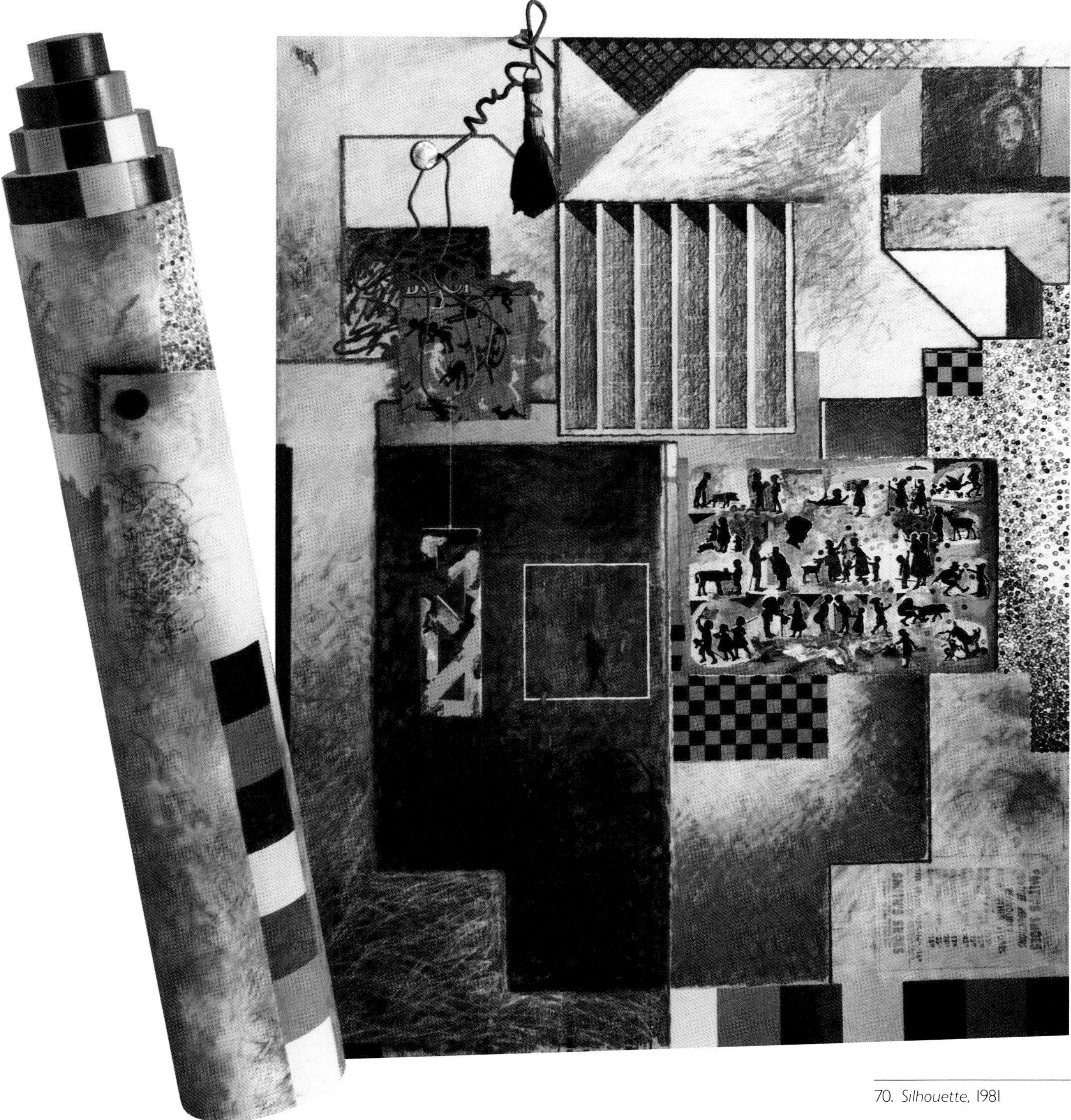

70. *Silhouette*, 1981

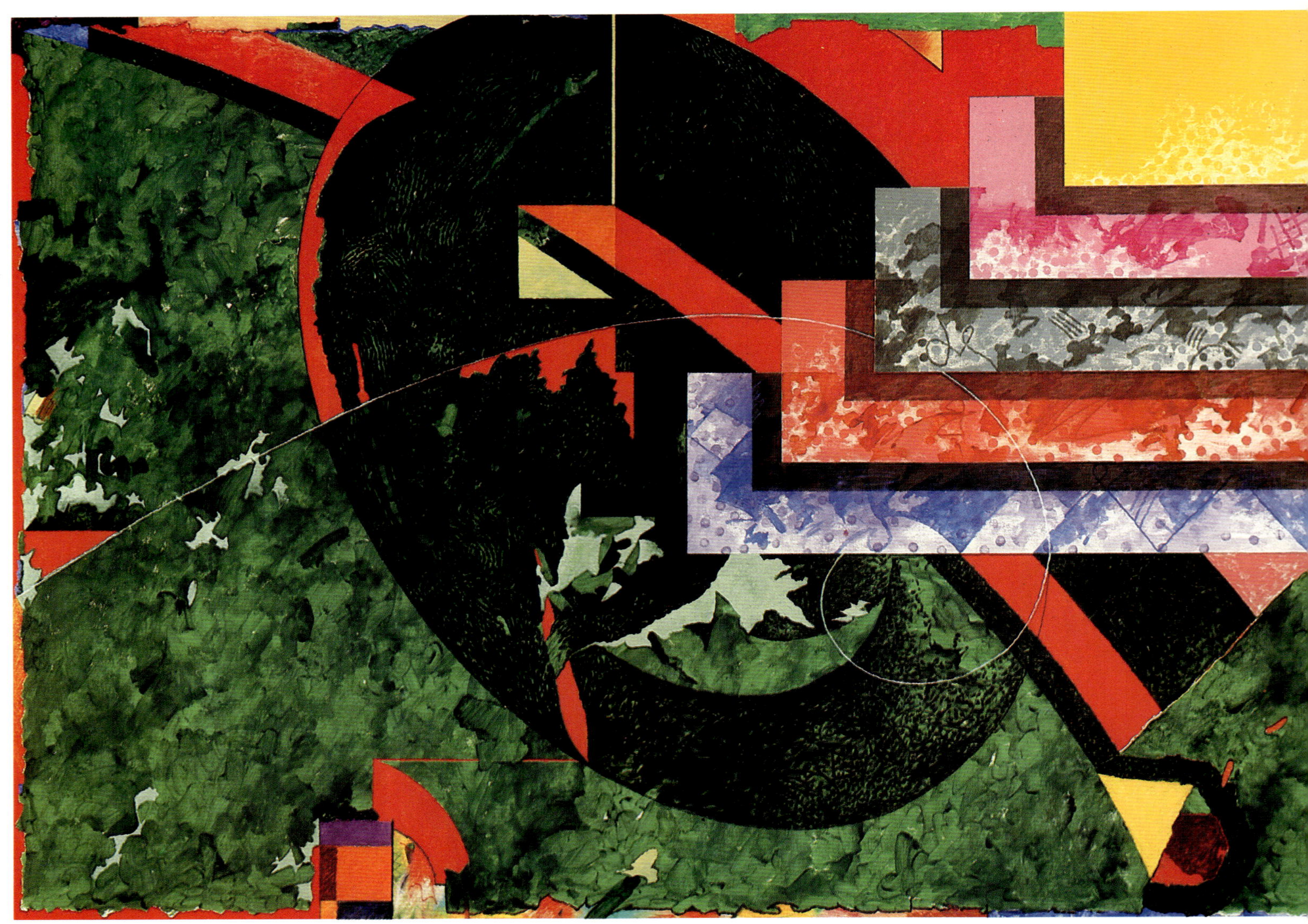

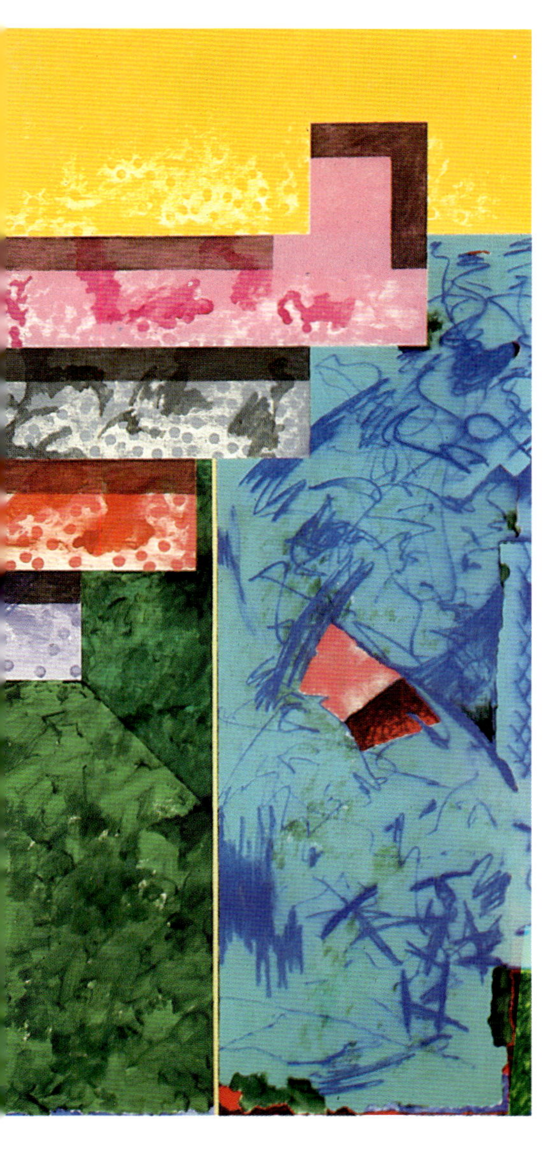

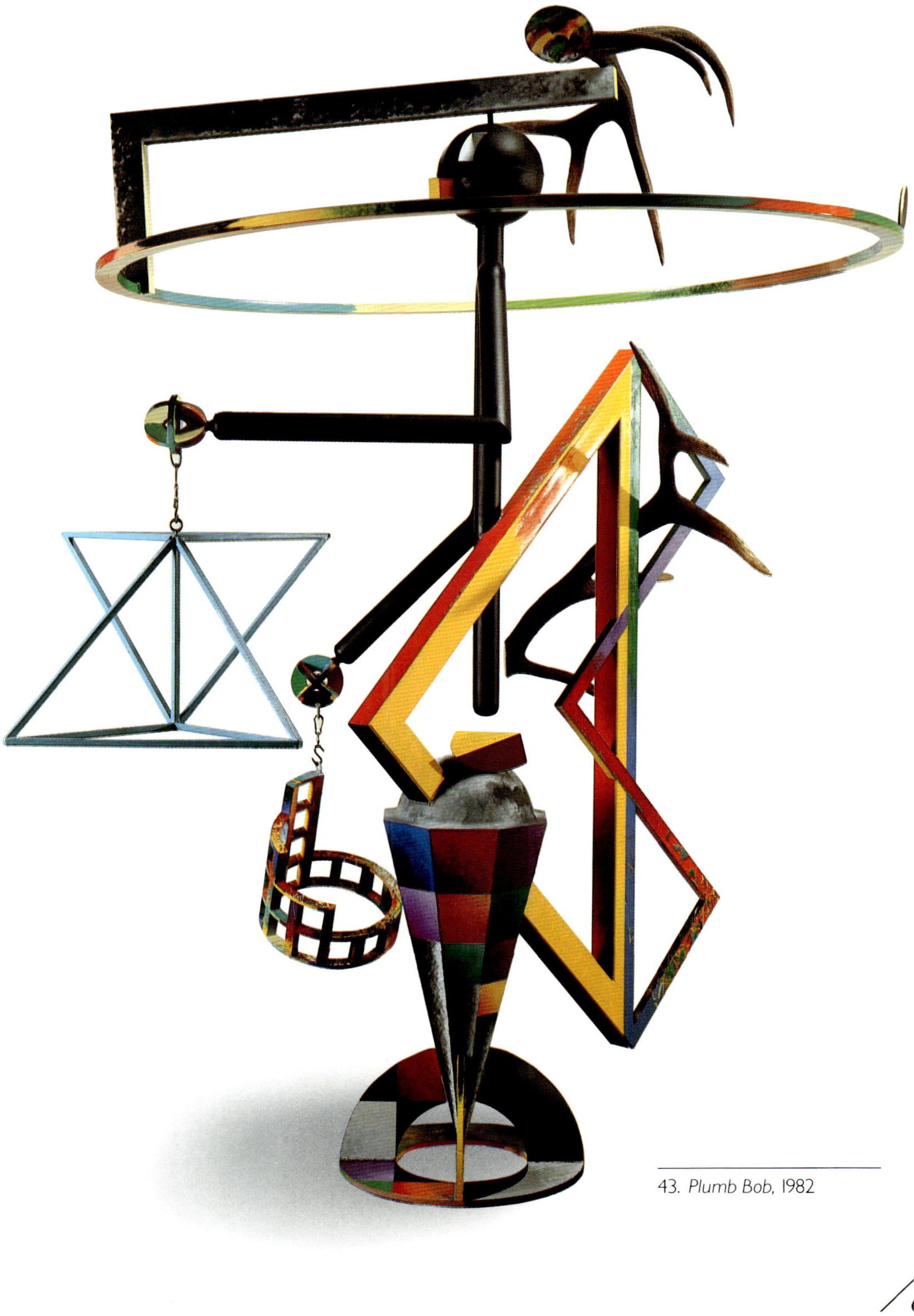

43. *Plumb Bob*, 1982

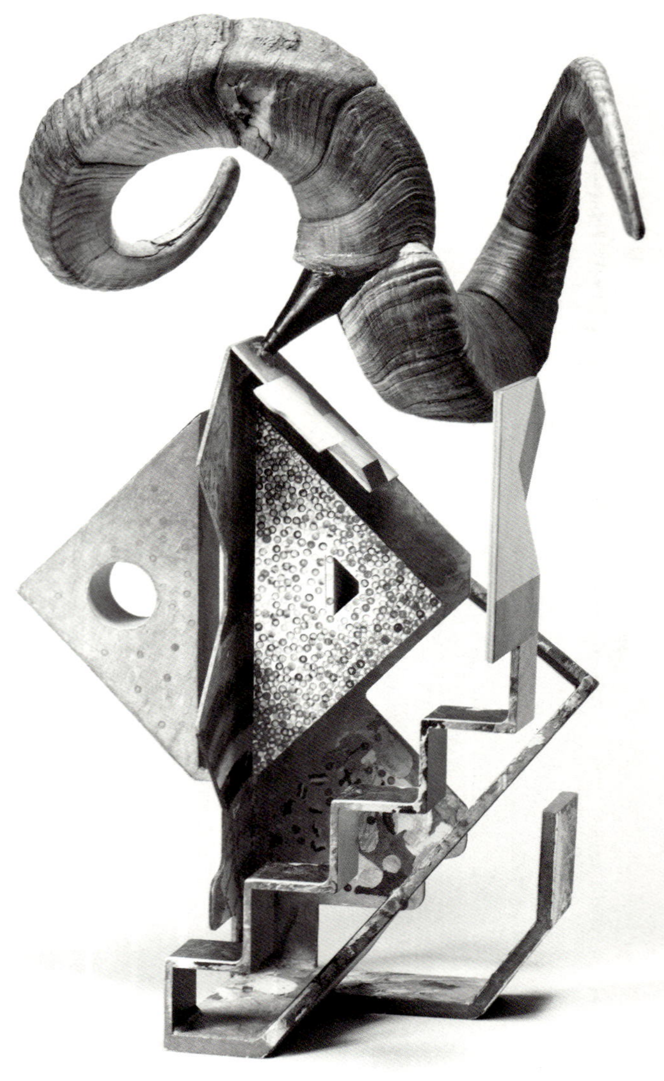

34. *By the Horns*, 1981

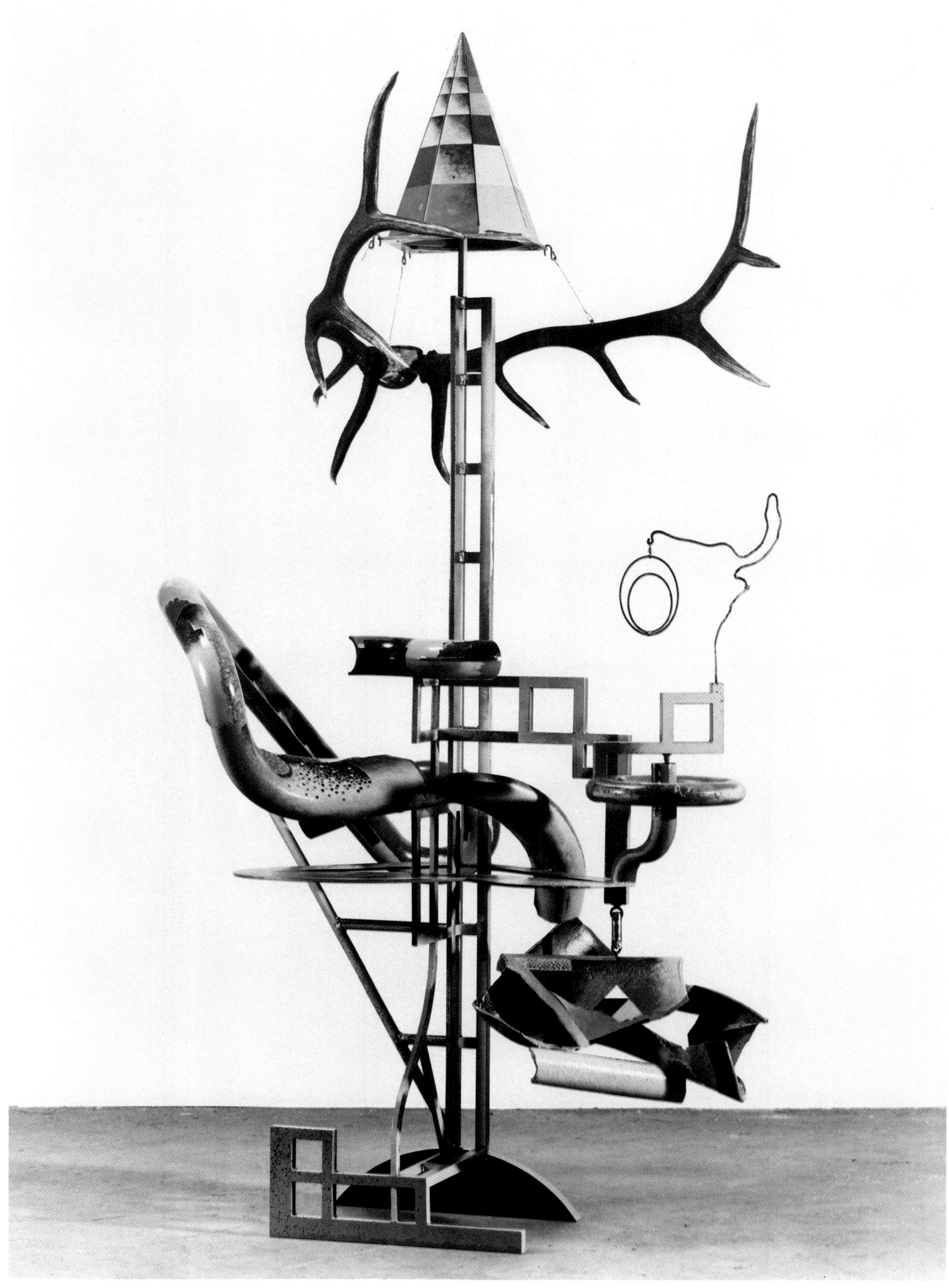

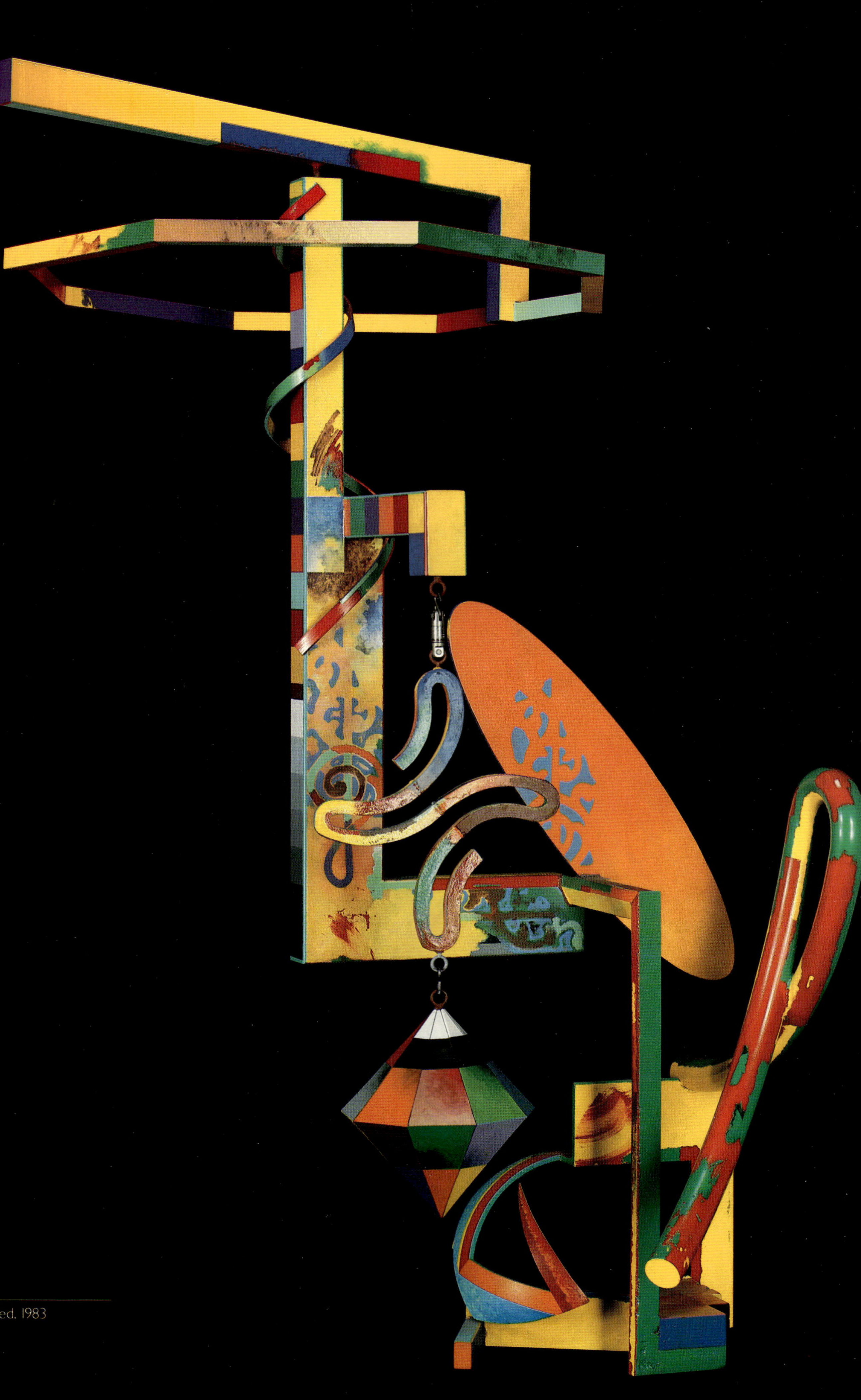

ed, 1983

Robert Hudson in his Stinson Beach Studio, California, 1965   photo: Jack Fulton

Robert Hudson with his son Cannon, 1967   photo: Jack Fulton

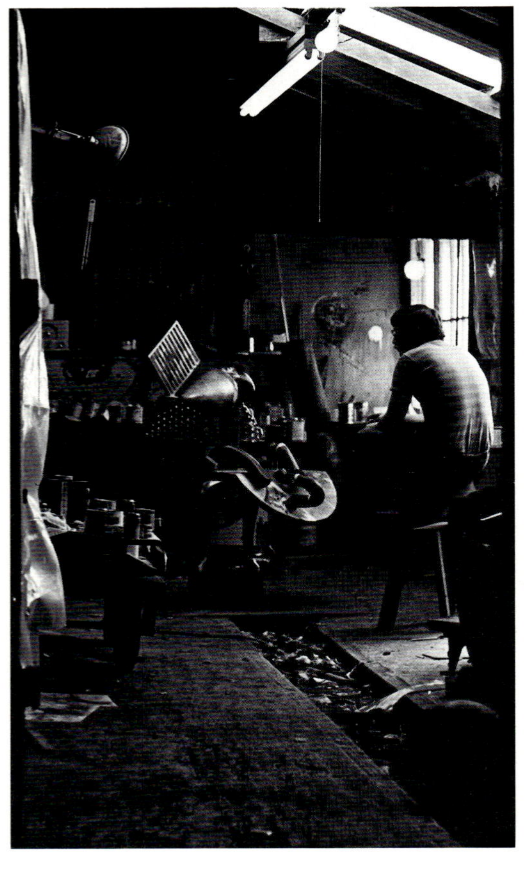

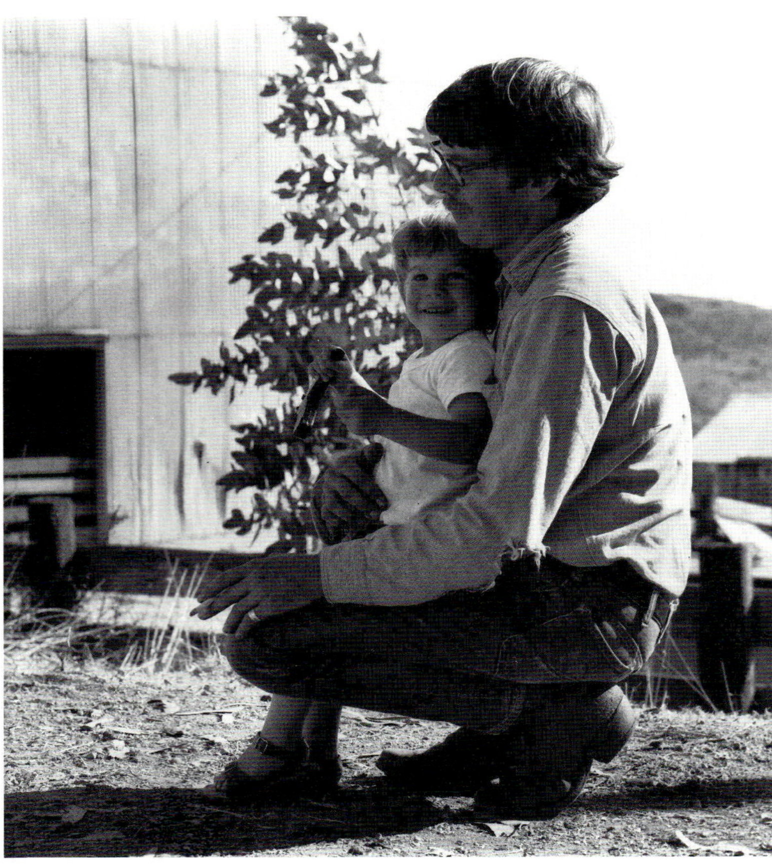

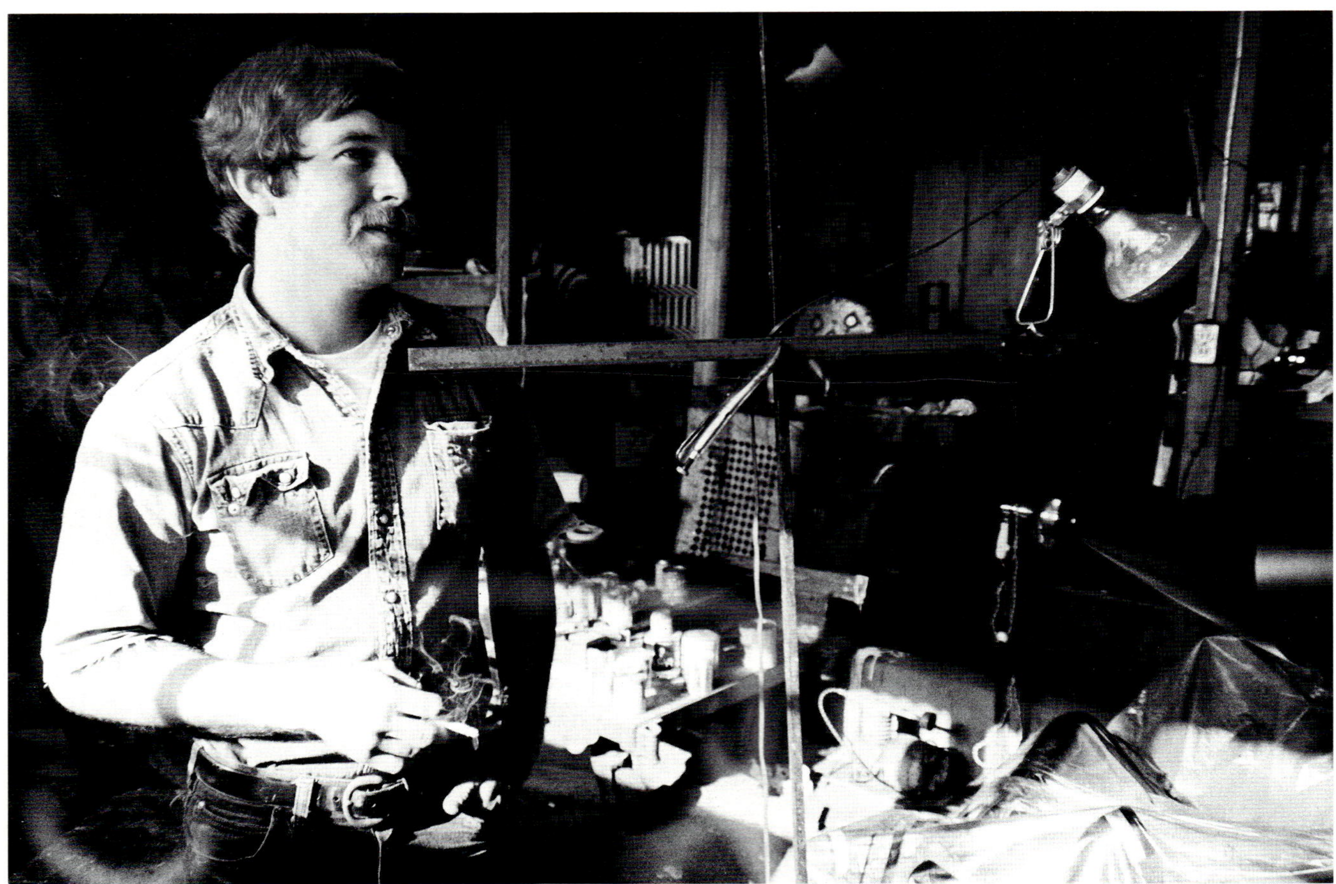

Robert Hudson, 1965   photo: Jack Fulton

Chronology

compiled by Michael Schwager

1938

Born 8 September in Salt Lake City.
Lives in Pioche, Nevada.

1944-47

Lives with family in different cities
throughout Pacific Northwest.

1948

Moves with family to Richland, Washington.

Meets William T. Wiley while in elementary
school.

1953

Enters Columbia High School in Richland.
Studies art with Jim McGrath.
Other students in McGrath's classes include
Wiley, William Allan, and William Witherup.

1957

Graduates from Columbia High School.
Enters California School of Fine Arts (now
the San Francisco Art Institute), to study
painting and sculpture. Instructors include
Nathan Oliveira, Frank Lobdell, Elmer
Bischoff, Jeremy Anderson, Gurdon Woods,
and Frank Hamilton.

1958

First exhibition at Green Gallery,
San Francisco. Exhibits sculpture
and drawings with Wiley.

1959

Works on stage sets for multi-media
performance entitled "The Event." Others
involved with project include Wiley,
Robert Nelson, Ron Davis, and members
of the San Francisco Mime Troup.

1961

Receives Bachelor of Fine Arts degree
from San Francisco Art Institute.

First solo exhibition at Batman Gallery,
San Francisco. Exhibits sculptures
and drawings.

1962

Marries Cornelia Schulz.

Moves to Bolinas, California, and sets
up studio there.

1963

Receives Master of Fine Arts from
San Francisco Art Institute.

Son Cannon Hudson born.

Moves to Stinson Beach, California, and sets
up studio there.

1964

Joins faculty of San Francisco Art Institute
as instructor of sculpture.

First show at Lanyon Gallery, Palo Alto,
California.

Included in *Annual Exhibition 1964:
Contemporary American Sculpture* at
Whitney Museum of American Art,
New York.

1965

Appointed Chairman of Sculpture/Ceramics
Department at San Francisco Art Institute.

Included in *Young American Sculpture—East
to West* exhibition at New York World's Fair.

Receives Nealie Sullivan Award,
San Francisco Art Institute.

First show at Allan Frumkin Gallery,
New York.

1966

Accepts position as Assistant Professor
of Art at University of California, Berkeley.
Other faculty members include Bischoff,
Peter Voulkos, James Melchert, Ron Nagle,
and Don Potts.

1967

Included in two important exhibitions:
Funk, at University Art Museum, University
of California, Berkeley, and *American
Sculpture of the Sixties* at Los Angeles County
Museum of Art.

1968

Son Case Hudson born.

1971

Begins working for first time in porcelain
with Richard Shaw in Shaw's studio
in Stinson Beach.

1972

Awarded Individual Artist Fellowship
from National Endowment for the Arts.

Moves to Mill Valley, California, and sets
up studio in Sausalito, California.

1973

Leaves teaching position at University
of California, Berkeley.

Exhibits porcelain work with Richard Shaw
at San Francisco Museum of Art.

Continues working on ceramics
and begins series of drawings and paintings
on cotton batting.

1974

Artist-in-Residence, University of Wisconsin,
Madison.

Guest lecturer, Maryland Institute, College
of Art, Baltimore, and Kansas City Art
Institute, Missouri.

1975

Takes part in first Artists' Soapbox Derby
sponsored by San Francisco Museum of Art.

Guest lecturer, University of California,
Berkeley.

Moves to Sausalito.

1976

Resumes teaching at San Francisco
Art Institute.

Marries Mavis Jukes.

Receives John Simon Guggenheim
Fellowship.

1977

Moves to Cotati, California. Uses money
from Guggenheim Fellowship to build
present studio.

Daughter River Jukes-Hudson born.

First survey exhibition organized by Moore
College of Art Gallery, Philadelphia.

1979

Awarded public sculpture commission under
the General Services Administration's
art-in-architecture program. Produced large
aluminum sculpture, *Tlingit,* for Federal
Building in Anchorage.

1980

Daughter Amy Jukes-Hudson born.

1982

Guest lecturer, Mills College, Oakland.

1983

Distinguished Visiting Professor, Department
of Art, University of California, Davis.

1984

Included in *California Sculpture Show,*
organized as part of 1984 Olympic
Arts Festival.

Travels to London and Bordeaux, France.

1985

Continues to live with family in Cotati,
California, and teach at San Francisco
Art Institute.

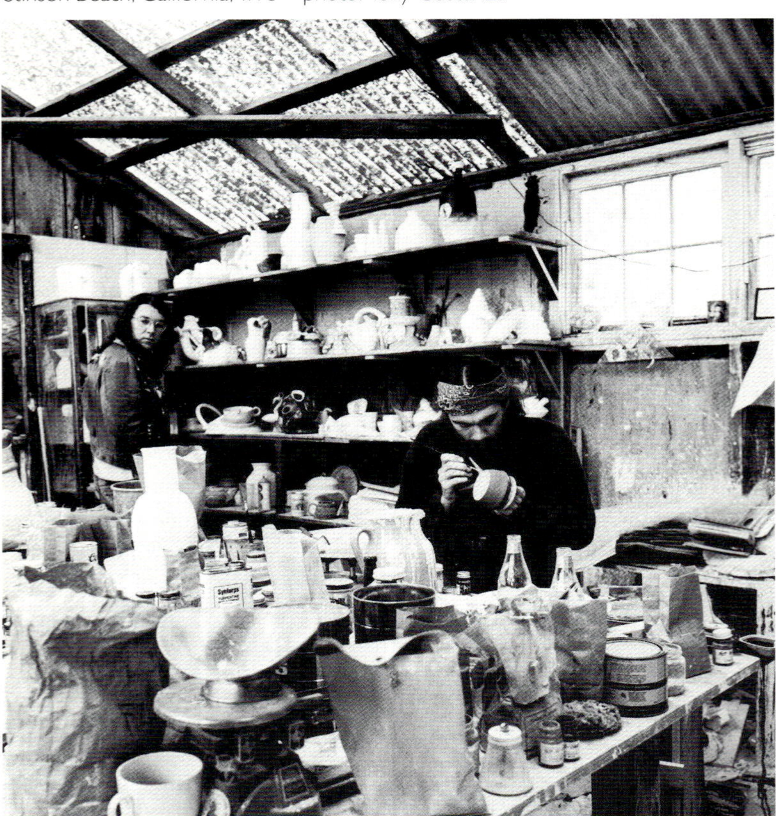
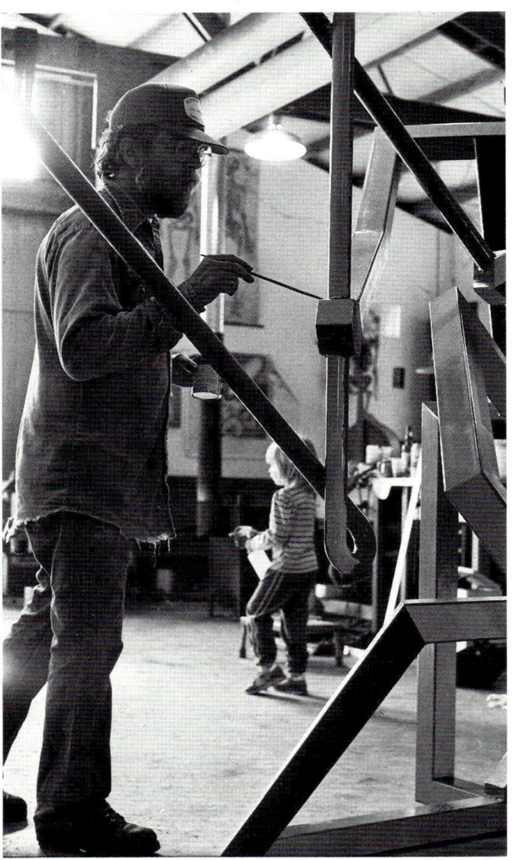

Robert Hudson (left) with Richard Shaw in Shaw's studio, Stinson Beach, California, 1973   photo: Tony Costanzo

Robert Hudson with his daughter Amy in his studio, Cotati, California, 1985   photo: John Montgomery

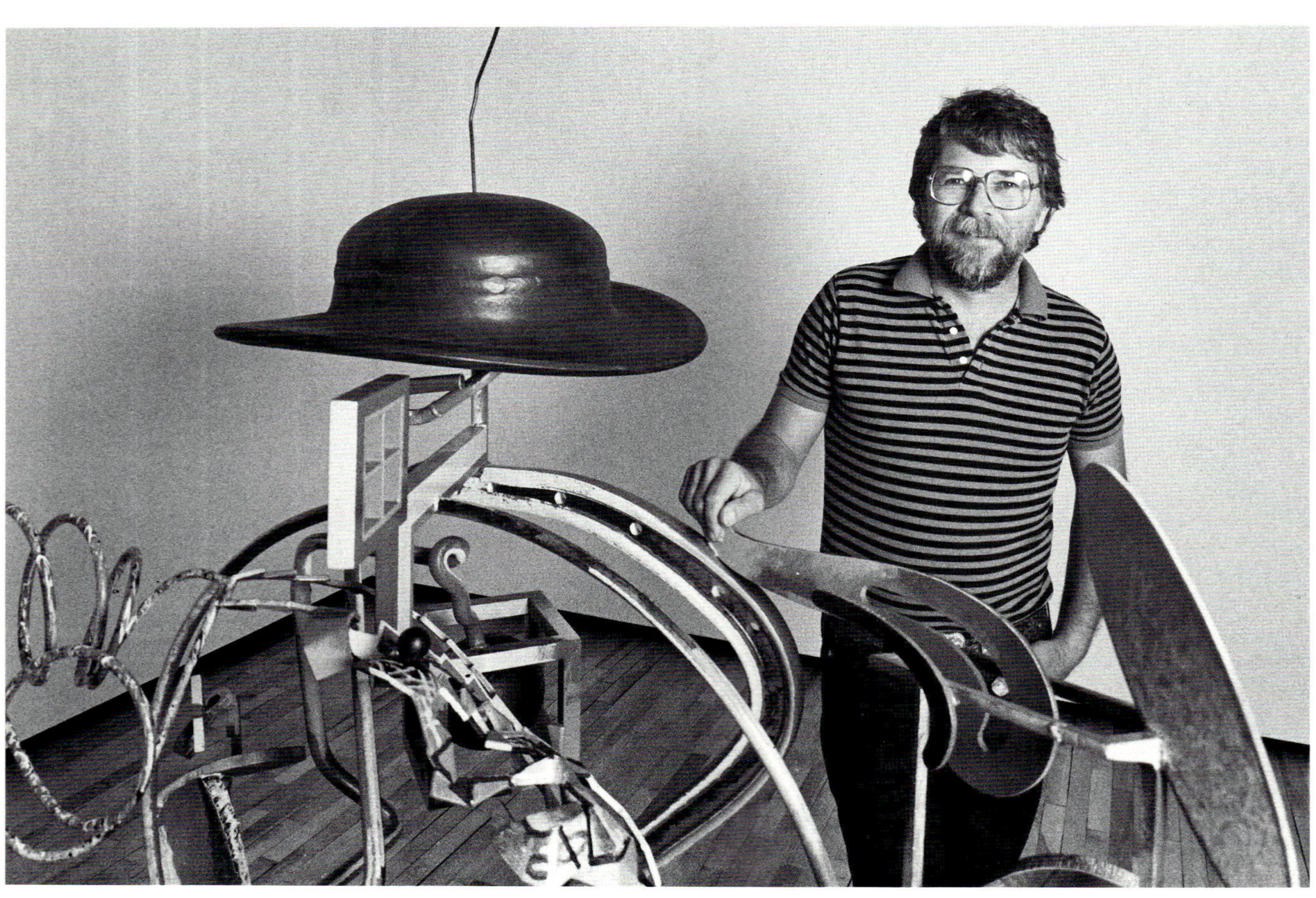

Robert Hudson with *Ear to Year*, 1984   photo: Harvey Stein

In the listing of dimensions, height precedes width precedes depth; centimeter measurements appear in parentheses. For works on paper, measurements indicate sheet size unless noted otherwise.

SCULPTURE

1. *Cannon,* 1960
enamel on steel, cast iron, aluminum
16 × 23 × 29" (40.6 × 58.4 × 73.7)
Manuel and Kate Neri, Benicia,
California

2. *Pipe Dream,* 1963
enamel on steel, cast iron
24 1/2 × 14 1/2 × 16 1/2" (62.2 × 36.8 × 41.9)
Byron Meyer, San Francisco

3. Untitled, 1963
enamel on steel, copper
96 × 65 × 40" (243.8 × 165.1 × 101.6)
Naomi and Robert Lauter,
San Francisco
(Will travel only to San Francisco)

4. *Blue Peen Hammer,* 1964
steel with enamel and lacquer
62 1/2 × 55 1/8 × 44" (158.7 × 140.3 × 111.8)
San Francisco Museum of Modern
Art, Gift of the Women's Board
64.69 A-B (Will travel only to
San Francisco)

5. *Diamond Back,* 1964
enamel on steel
74 × 57 × 35" (188.0 × 144.8 × 129.5)
Private collection, New York

6. *Fat Knat,* 1964
enamel on steel
55 1/8 × 17 1/2 × 53 7/8" (139.9 × 44.5 × 136.7)
The Museum of Modern Art,
New York, Fractional gift
of Charles Cowles, 1973

7. *Inside Out,* 1964
enamel on steel
104 × 62 × 36" (264.2 × 157.5 × 91.4)
Matthew D. and Wanda Ashe,
Sausalito, California

8. *Log Boot,* 1964
enamel on steel
32 × 21 × 14" (81.3 × 53.3 × 36.6)
Nicholas Wilder, New York

9. *Skylight,* 1964
enamel on steel
74 × 34 × 24" (188.0 × 86.4 × 61.0)
Dr. and Mrs. William R. Fielder,
Atherton, California

10. *T Table,* 1964
enamel and lacquer on steel
54 × 36 × 36" (137.2 × 91.4 × 91.4)
Audrey Sabol, Key Largo, Florida

11. *Skeptical Space,* 1965
enamel on steel
45 × 32 × 30" (114.3 × 81.3 × 76.2)
Dr. and Mrs. Gerald Bush, Concord,
Massachusetts
(Will travel only to San Francisco)

12. Untitled, 1965
enamel and lacquer on steel
66 × 48 × 43" (167.6 × 121.9 × 109.2)
Mr. and Mrs. C. David Robinson,
Sausalito, California

13. *Space Window,* 1966
automobile lacquer on steel
69 × 60 × 57" (175.2 × 152.4 × 144.8)
Sally Lilienthal, San Francisco
(Will travel only to San Francisco
and Buffalo)

14. *Space Wrap with a Western Cut,* 1966
enamel on steel, plastic
68 × 83 × 42" (172.7 × 210.8 × 106.7)
Mr. and Mrs. William Wilson III,
Hillsborough, California

15. *Twisted Hip,* 1967
enamel and chrome plating on steel
and aluminum
180 × 84 × 84" (457.2 × 213.4 × 213.4)
Rene and Veronica di Rosa,
Napa, California

16. *Black Lift,* 1968
lacquer on steel and aluminum
85 × 64 × 58" (215.9 × 162.6 × 147.3)
Philadelphia Museum of Art,
Anonymous gift in honor
of Anne d'Harnoncourt
(Will travel only to San Francisco
and Buffalo)

17. *4 x 4,* 1968
lacquer on steel
19 7/8 × 11 × 20 1/2" (50.5 × 28.0 × 52.1)
The Art Institute of Chicago,
Gift of the Robert A. Lewis Fund
in memory of William and Polly Levey

18. *Skeleton,* 1969-84
lacquer on bone and glass,
chrome-plated steel
81 3/4 × 26 1/2 × 22" (207.6 × 67.3 × 55.9)
Robert Hudson and Mavis Jukes,
Cotati, California

19. *Dream,* 1970
oak, aluminum, steel thermometer,
plastic
35 1/2 × 24 1/2 × 180" (90.2 × 62.2 × 457.2)
Robert Hudson and Mavis Jukes,
Cotati, California

20. *Still Works,* 1970
glass, bronze, aluminum, arc welder
29 1/2 × 31 1/2 × 49 3/4" (74.9 × 79.8 × 126.4)
Robert Hudson and Mavis Jukes,
Cotati, California
(Will travel only to San Francisco)

21. *True Blue,* 1970
zinc coating and baked
epoxy on steel
79 1/2 × 48 1/2 × 176" (201.9 × 123.9 × 447.0)
Robert Hudson and Mavis Jukes,
Cotati, California

22. *Cowboy Star,* 1971
enamel on steel, chains, decal
33 3/8 × 45 1/2" (84.8 × 115.6)
University Art Museum,
University of California, Berkeley,
Gift of Mr. and Mrs. Philip Lilienthal

23. *Whip,* 1971
acrylic on wood, steel, vinyl,
plasticine clay
82 × 48 × 12" (208.3 × 121.9 × 30.5)
Courtesy Allan Frumkin Gallery,
New York
(Will travel only to San Francisco)

24. *Window Star,* 1971
enamel on aluminum
44 × 46" (111.8 × 116.8)
Wellington Management/Thorndike,
Doran, Paine, and Lewis, Boston
(Will travel only to San Francisco)

25. *Stacked Deck,* 1972
stainless steel, rubber, Plexiglas
21 × 48 1/4 × 36 3/4" (53.3 × 122.5 × 93.3)
Mavis Jukes, Cotati, California

26. *Cowboy Saddle Light,* 1974
wood, canvas, glass, aluminum,
bowling ball, cowboy hat, wooden
stool, chains, found objects
91 × 41 × 28" (231.1 × 104.1 × 71.1)
Mr. and Mrs. Marvin Singer, Atlanta

27. Untitled, 1974-81
acrylic on aluminum
32 × 23" (81.2 × 58.4)
Rene and Veronica di Rosa,
Napa, California

28. *Running through the Woods,* 1975
stuffed deer, wood, rock, globe,
metal, string, feathers,
found objects, acrylic
77 × 62 × 50 3/4" (195.6 × 157.5 × 128.9)
Mr. and Mrs. C. David Robinson,
Sausalito, California

29. *Daddy's Apron Strings,* 1976
carpenter's apron, plastic, wire,
feather, acrylic, charcoal
52 × 23 × 9" (132.1 × 58.4 × 22.9)
Dorothy A. Goldeen, San Francisco
(Will travel only to San Francisco)

30. *Five in Disguise,* 1976
cardboard, glass, wire, plastic
32 × 50 × 28" (81.3 × 127.0 × 71.1)
Jane and Ruth Root
(Will travel only to San Francisco)

31. *Kachina,* 1976
wood, plastic dice, stainless steel,
whisk broom figure, bronze, steel
globe, rock, feathers, found objects
48 × 48 × 18 1/2" (121.9 × 121.9 × 47.0)
Stedelijk Museum, Amsterdam
(Will travel only to San Francisco
and Buffalo)

32. *Dad Goes to Work,* 1977
glass, plastic, masonite, wood,
acrylic, wire
40 × 15 × 15" (101.6 × 38.1 × 38.1)
William T. Wiley, California

33. *Dead Pan Expression*, 1977
steel, bowling ball, rubber, bone,
wood, fabric, string, chains, pots, pans
52 × 38 × 31" (132.1 × 96.5 × 78.7)
Don and Nancy Eiler,
Madison, Wisconsin

34. *By the Horns*, 1981
acrylic on steel, ram's horn
31 × 19 × 20" (78.7 × 48.3 × 50.8)
Rene and Veronica di Rosa,
Napa, California

35. *Balance Point*, 1982
pastel on steel, plastic coating,
moose antlers, ram's horn
84 × 52 × 34" (213.4 × 132.1 × 86.4)
Rene and Veronica di Rosa,
Napa, California

36. *Blue Z*, 1982
enamel on steel, cast iron, chain
45 × 31 × 20" (114.3 × 78.7 × 50.8)
Hamilton-Wells Collection,
San Francisco

37. *Brushstroke*, 1982
wood guitar, paintbrush, clock spring,
acrylic on wood, false teeth
35 × 23 × 14" (88.9 × 58.4 × 35.6)
Robert Hudson and Mavis Jukes,
Cotati, California

38. *Face to Face*, 1982
enamel on steel, copper
38 × 28 × 23" (96.5 × 71.1 × 58.4)
Byron Meyer, San Francisco

39. *Grin*, 1982
enamel on steel, reindeer antlers,
wire, metal bar tray
43½ × 36 × 20" (110.5 × 92.7 × 52.7)
Dorothy A. Goldeen, San Francisco

40. *Hot Water*, 1982
steel with enamel, acrylic,
and metal teapot
91 × 36 × 53" (231.1 × 91.4 × 134.6)
San Francisco Museum of Modern
Art, Purchased with the aid of
funds from Rene di Rosa and an
anonymous donor 83.24 A-E

41. *Iron Dancer*, 1982
enamel on steel, acrylic, cast iron,
tin, antler
66 × 63 × 26" (167.6 × 160.0 × 66.0)
Robert Hudson and Mavis Jukes,
Cotati, California
(Will travel only to San Francisco)

42. *Moon Rock*, 1982
enamel on steel and cast iron
36 × 20 × 8" (91.4 × 50.8 × 20.3)
Mr. and Mrs. Edmund Nash,
Belvedere, California
(Will travel only to San Francisco)

43. *Plumb Bob*, 1982
enamel on steel, antlers, mirror
102½ × 82½ × 72¼"
(260.3 × 209.5 × 183.5)
Mr. and Mrs. Harry W. Anderson,
Atherton, California
(Will travel only to San Francisco
and Buffalo)

44. *Steel Kachina*, 1982
enamel and acrylic on steel
33 × 23 × 17" (83.8 × 58.4 × 43.2)
Mr. and Mrs. C. David Robinson,
Sausalito, California
(Will travel only to San Francisco)

45. Untitled, 1982
enamel on steel
29 × 28 × 28" (73.7 × 71.1 × 71.1)
Robert Arneson and Sandra
Shannonhouse, Benicia, California

46. *Dog Leg*, 1983
enamel on steel, cast iron
31½ × 23 × 11" (80.0 × 58.4 × 27.9)
Martin Sklar, New York

47. Untitled, 1983
enamel on steel
89 × 58 × 36½" (226.1 × 147.3 × 92.7)
Museum of Fine Arts, Boston,
Special Paintings Fund
(Will travel only to San Francisco)

48. *Ear to Year*, 1983-84
enamel on steel, cast iron, nylon scarf
97 × 71 × 57" (246.4 × 180.3 × 144.8)
Courtesy Allan Frumkin Gallery,
New York

49. *Homage to Miró*, 1983-84
enamel on steel, bronze, cast iron
86 × 58 × 36" (218.4 × 147.3 × 91.4)
Laura-Lee Woods, Los Angeles

50. *Outrigger*, 1983-84
enamel on steel, cast iron, antlers
107 × 37 × 54" (269.2 × 94.0 × 137.2)
Courtesy Allan Frumkin Gallery,
New York

51. *Painting*, 1983-84
enamel on steel
74 × 37 × 33" (188.0 × 94.0 × 83.8)
Laila and Thurston Twigg-Smith,
Honolulu

PAINTINGS

52. *Untitled III*, 1973
acrylic, pastel, charcoal
on cotton batting
75 × 95¾" (190.5 × 243.2)
Rene and Veronica di Rosa,
Napa, California

53. *Love Lock*, 1974
acrylic, pastel, charcoal on canvas
68 × 72" (172.7 × 182.9)
Mr. and Mrs. Edmund Nash,
Belvedere, California
(Will travel only to San Francisco)

54. Untitled, 1975
acrylic, pastel, charcoal on cotton
batting, steel globe
75 × 96 × 12" (190.5 × 243.8 × 30.5)
Atlantic Richfield Company Corporate
Art Collection, Los Angeles

55. *Bear Claw*, 1976
acrylic, pastel, charcoal on canvas
66¼ × 48¼" (168.3 × 122.6)
Hamilton-Wells Collection,
San Francisco

56. *Indian Woman*, 1976
acrylic, pastel, charcoal
on cotton batting
74 × 75" (188.0 × 190.5)
Byron Meyer, San Francisco

57. *Kiva*, 1976
acrylic, pastel, charcoal on canvas
67 × 59" (170.2 × 149.9)
Mr. and Mrs. Graham Gund

58. *Rocky Hill*, 1976
acrylic, pastel, charcoal
on cotton batting
74 × 150½" (188.0 × 382.3)
Courtesy Allan Frumkin Gallery,
New York

59. Untitled, 1976
acrylic, pastel, charcoal on cotton
batting, with cowboy hat, wood,
thread, canvas, aluminum
74 × 152 × 40" (188.0 × 386.1 × 101.6)
Adam Aronson, St. Louis

60. *K-6*, 1977
acrylic, pastel, charcoal on canvas,
with plastic, steel, wooden chair,
wooden boat, glass
104 × 158 × 40" (264.2 × 401.3 × 101.6)
Mr. and Mrs. Graham Gund

61. *Spur of the Moment*, 1977
acrylic, pastel, charcoal on canvas,
with canvas strapping, wood, beads,
metal bucket, steel mirror, plastic hand,
fishing creel, twigs, silver spur
86 × 63 × 25" (218.4 × 160.0 × 63.5)
Mr. and Mrs. Graham Gund

62. *After Image*, 1978
acrylic, charcoal on canvas
84 × 84" (213.4 × 213.4)
Robert Hudson and Mavis Jukes,
Cotati, California;
Courtesy Fuller Goldeen Gallery,
San Francisco, and Allan Frumkin
Gallery, New York

63. *Eye Beam*, 1978
acrylic, pastel, charcoal on canvas
81½ × 154" (207.0 × 391.2)
Mr. and Mrs. Graham Gund

64. *Indian Woman II*, 1978
acrylic, pastel, charcoal,
collage on canvas
48 × 84" (121.9 × 213.4)
Alice and Martin Grossman,
M.D., Miami Beach
(Will travel only to San Francisco)

65. Untitled, 1978
acrylic on canvas
84 × 84" (213.4 × 213.4)
Robert Hudson and Mavis Jukes,
Cotati, California;
Courtesy Fuller Goldeen Gallery,
San Francisco, and Allan Frumkin
Gallery, New York

66. *Figure Painting,* 1980
acrylic, pastel, charcoal on canvas
with wood, cast paper, fiberglass,
Canadian currency, rubber bicycle
tire, wire
76 × 42 × 21″ (193.0 × 116.8 × 53.3)
Jerome and Margaret Nerman,
Kansas City, Missouri

67. Untitled, 1980
acrylic, pastel on canvas with wood,
wire, clock spring, rock, feathers,
steel globe, paint brush, collage
56 × 44 × 32″ (142.2 × 111.8 × 81.3)
Rene and Veronica di Rosa,
Napa, California

68. *Out of the Blue,* 1980-81
acrylic on canvas with wooden chair,
plastic tree, wood, and steel tubing
96³⁄₈ × 180⁷⁄₈ × 27³⁄₄″
(244.8 × 459.4 × 70.5)
San Francisco Museum of Modern
Art, Purchased with the aid of the
Byron Meyer Fund 81.57 A-D (Will
travel only to San Francisco)

69. Untitled, 1980-81
acrylic, charcoal, enamel paint, collage
on canvas, wood, masonite, tin,
finishing saw, wire
76 × 46 × 21″ (193.0 × 116.8 × 53.3)
Rene and Veronica di Rosa,
Napa, California

70. *Silhouette,* 1981
acrylic, pastel, charcoal, wood, wire,
collage on canvas
56¹⁄₄ × 54 × 16″ (142.9 × 137.2 × 40.6)
Private collection

71. *Art Felt Swoop,* 1982
acrylic, pastel, charcoal on canvas
74³⁄₄ × 61³⁄₄″ (189.9 × 154.9)
Private collection

DRAWINGS

72. Untitled, 1974
acrylic, pastel, charcoal on paper
30¹⁄₂ × 25¹⁄₂″ (77.5 × 64.8)
Wayne Andersen, Boston

73. Untitled, 1974
acrylic, pastel, graphite,
charcoal on paper
30¹⁄₂ × 25¹⁄₂″ (77.5 × 64.8)
Mr. and Mrs. C. David Robinson,
Sausalito, California

74. Untitled, 1974
acrylic, pastel, graphite, charcoal,
collage on paper
25¹⁄₂ × 30¹⁄₂″ (64.8 × 77.4)
Robert Hudson and Mavis Jukes,
Cotati, California

75. Untitled, 1974
acrylic, pastel, charcoal on paper
14 × 22″ (35.6 × 55.9)
Patrick Brennan, San Francisco
(Will travel only to San Francisco)

76. Untitled, 1975
acrylic, pastel, charcoal on paper
30¹⁄₂ × 25¹⁄₂″ (77.4 × 64.8)
Deborah Allen, Medford, New Jersey

77. Untitled, 1975
acrylic, pastel, charcoal, feather, plastic
netting, safety pins, cloth, thread,
wood on paper
32 × 26 × 2″ (81.3 × 66.0 × 5.1)
Rene and Veronica di Rosa,
Napa, California
(Will travel only to San Francisco)

78. *Round-Up,* 1976
acrylic, pastel, charcoal,
collage on paper
32¹⁄₁₆ × 42¹⁄₁₆″ (81.4 × 106.8)
Mrs. Ralph J. Mills, Jr., Chicago
(Will travel only to San Francisco)

79. Untitled, 1977
acrylic, pastel, charcoal,
collage on paper
42 × 55″ (106.7 × 139.7)
Wally Goodman, San Francisco

80. Untitled, 1977
acrylic, pastel, charcoal,
collage on paper
32 × 42″ (81.3 × 106.7)
James Cottrell, New York

81. Untitled, 1977
acrylic, pastel, charcoal,
collage on paper
30 × 25″ (76.2 × 63.5)
W. Scott Woods, San Francisco
(Will travel only to San Francisco)

82. Untitled, 1977
acrylic, pastel, charcoal,
collage on paper
30 × 25″ (76.2 × 63.5)
Stephen S. Alpert Family Trust
(Will travel only to San Francisco)

83. *Black Widow,* 1978
acrylic, pastel, charcoal on paper
42 × 32″ (106.7 × 81.3)
Robert Gordy, New Orleans
(Will travel only to San Francisco)

84. *Drumhead,* 1978
acrylic, collage on paper
42 × 32″ (106.7 × 81.3)
Diana Fuller, San Francisco

85. *For Milady's Coiffure,* 1978
acrylic, pastel, collage on paper
32 × 42″ (81.3 × 106.7)
Jim Proby, San Francisco

86. *Longhorn,* 1978
acrylic, charcoal, collage on paper
32 × 42″ (81.3 × 106.7)
Security Pacific Bank Corporate
Collection, Los Angeles
(Will travel only to San Francisco)

87. *Portrait,* 1978
acrylic, pastel, charcoal, graphite,
enamel spray paint, collage on paper
32 × 42″ (81.3 × 106.7)
Mr. and Mrs. Graham Gund

88. *Look,* 1979
acrylic, pastel, collage,
enamel paint on paper
32 × 42″ (81.3 × 106.7)
Courtesy Fuller Goldeen Gallery,
San Francisco

89. Untitled, 1979
acrylic, pastel, charcoal, collage, safety
pins on paper
30 × 67³⁄₄″ (76.2 × 172.1)
Private collection

90. Untitled, 1979
acrylic, charcoal, graphite, collage,
safety pins on paper
42 × 32″ (106.7 × 81.3)
Private collection
(Will travel only to San Francisco)

91. Untitled, 1979
acrylic, pastel, charcoal, enamel spray
paint on paper
42 × 63″ (106.7 × 160.0)
Stephen S. Alpert Family Trust

92. Untitled, 1979
acrylic, pastel, charcoal,
collage on paper
42 × 95¹⁄₄″ (106.7 × 241.9)
Byron Meyer, San Francisco

93. Untitled, 1980
acrylic, pastel, charcoal, paper fan,
collage on paper
42¹⁄₁₆ × 32¹⁄₁₆″ (106.8 × 81.4)
Wayne E. Campbell and
Richard S. Canter, New York

94. Untitled, 1980
acrylic, pastel, charcoal, graphite,
paper fan, collage on paper
42 × 32″ (106.7 × 81.3)
Private collection, New York

95. Untitled, 1980
acrylic, pastel, enamel paint,
paper fan, collage on paper
42 × 32″ (106.7 × 81.3)
Courtesy Allan Frumkin Gallery,
New York

96. Untitled, 1980
acrylic, enamel paint, paper fan,
collage on paper
42 × 32″ (106.7 × 81.3)
Courtesy Frumkin & Struve Gallery,
Chicago
(Will travel only to San Francisco)

97. Untitled, 1980
acrylic, pastel, charcoal, graphite,
paper fan, collage on paper
42 × 32″ (106.7 × 81.3)
The Prudential Insurance Company
of America, Newark, New Jersey

98. Untitled, 1980
acrylic, pastel, charcoal, graphite,
paper fan, collage on paper
42 × 32″ (106.7 × 81.3)
Jack and Rena Thompson,
Chalfont, Pennsylvania

99.   Untitled, 1980
       acrylic, pastel, charcoal, graphite,
       paper fan, collage on paper
       42 × 32″ (106.7 × 81.3)
       Wright/Bonfilio, San Francisco
       (Will travel only to San Francisco)

100.   Untitled, 1980
       acrylic, pastel, charcoal, graphite,
       paper fan, collage on paper
       42 × 32″ (106.7 × 81.3)
       John and Mary Pappajohn,
       Des Moines

101.   Untitled, 1982
       printers ink, oil collage, cast paper,
       safety pins on paper
       31 × 50 × 5″ (78.7 × 127.0 × 12.7)
       The Capital Group, Inc., Los Angeles
       (Will travel only to San Francisco)

CERAMICS

102.   Bottle, 1972
       porcelain with underglazes
       and china paint
       16½ × 7¼ × 5½″ (41.9 × 18.4 × 14.0)
       Peter Voulkos, Oakland

103.   Cup, 1972
       porcelain with underglazes
       and china paint
       5¾ × 5¼ × 3¼″ (14.6 × 13.3 × 8.3)
       Richard and Martha Shaw,
       Fairfax, California

104.   Jar, 1972
       porcelain with underglazes
       and china paint
       8 × 7 × 7″ (20.3 × 17.8 × 17.8)
       Mr. and Mrs. C. David Robinson,
       Sausalito, California

105.   Jar, 1972
       porcelain with underglazes
       and china paint
       12 × 12 × 9½″ (30.5 × 30.5 × 24.1)
       Mr. and Mrs. Edmund Nash,
       Belvedere California
       (Will travel only to San Francisco)

106.   Jar, 1972
       porcelain with underglazes
       and china paint
       16 × 11 × 8¼″ (40.6 × 27.9 × 20.9)
       Daniel Jacobs, New York

107.   Jar, 1972-73
       porcelain with underglazes
       and china paint
       13¼ × 9 × 10″ (33.7 × 22.9 × 25.4)
       Byron Meyer, San Francisco
       (Will travel only to San Francisco)

108.   Teapot, 1972
       porcelain with underglazes
       and china paint
       17½ × 12½ × 8½″ (44.4 × 31.7 × 21.6)
       Rene and Veronica di Rosa,
       Napa, California

109.   Teapot, 1972
       porcelain with underglazes
       and china paint
       13¼ × 16 × 12½″ (33.6 × 40.6 × 31.7)
       Mr. and Mrs. John Lowell Jones,
       Stinson Beach, California
       (Will travel only to San Francisco)

110.   Bottle, 1973
       porcelain with underglazes, china
       paint, quartz crystal, cork
       8¼ × 6¾ × 4½″ (20.9 × 17.1 × 11.4)
       Robert Arneson and Sandra
       Shannonhouse, Benicia, California

111.   Bottle, 1973
       porcelain with underglazes
       and china paint
       13½ × 11¼ × 7½″ (34.2 × 28.6 × 19.0)
       Dr. and Mrs. Harold J. Joseph,
       St. Louis
       (Will travel only to San Francisco)

112.   Bowl, 1973
       porcelain with underglazes, china
       paint, tin star, leather, wood, thread
       17½ × 12 × 9½″ (44.4 × 30.5 × 49.5)
       Central Iowa Art Association,
       Marshalltown

113.   Cup, 1973
       porcelain with underglazes
       and china paint
       3½ × 7 × 3½″ (8.9 × 17.8 × 8.9)
       Mr. and Mrs. William Wilson III,
       Hillsborough, California
       (Will travel only to San Francisco)

114.   Indian Pot, 1973
       porcelain with underglazes, china
       paint, feathers, sterling silver star,
       leather, thread
       15¼ × 10 × 6½″ (38.7 × 25.4 × 16.5)
       Matthew D. and Wanda Ashe,
       Sausalito, California

115.   Teapot, 1973
       porcelain with underglazes
       and china paint
       8½ × 13¾ × 5⅜″ (21.6 × 34.9 × 13.7)
       San Francisco Museum of Modern Art,
       William L. Gerstle Collection,
       William L. Gerstle Fund Purchase
       73.49

116.   Bottle, 1974
       porcelain with underglazes
       and china paint
       16½ × 9¾ × 9¾″ (41.9 × 24.8 × 24.8)
       Dorothy A. Goldeen, San Francisco
       (Will travel only to San Francisco)

117.   Cup, 1974
       porcelain with underglazes
       and china paint
       4 × 5 × 4″ (10.2 × 12.7 × 10.2)
       Dr. and Mrs. William R. Fielder,
       Atherton, California
       (Will travel only to San Francisco)

118.   Teapot, 1974
       porcelain with underglazes
       and china paint
       8¾ × 8 × 3½″ (22.2 × 20.3 × 8.9)
       William T. Wiley, California
       (Will travel only to San Francisco)

Exhibition History

compiled by Michael Schwager

SOLO EXHIBITIONS

1961

Batman Gallery, San Francisco.
Sculpture and Drawings by Robert Hudson.
7 June–2 July 1961.

Richmond Art Center, California.
Sculpture by Robert Hudson. 5–30 July 1961.

1962

Bolles Gallery, San Francisco. *Robert Hudson.*
8 January–3 February 1962.

1964

Lanyon Gallery, Palo Alto, California.
Robert Hudson. 4–31 October 1964.

1965

Diego Rivera Gallery, San Francisco Art
Institute. *Robert Hudson Sculpture:
1965 Nealie Sullivan Award Exhibition.*
1–21 September 1965.

Allan Frumkin Gallery, New York.
Robert Hudson: First New York Exhibition.
5–30 October 1965.

1967

Nicholas Wilder Gallery, Los Angeles.
Robert Hudson: Recent Sculpture.
26 September–14 October 1967.

1970

Michael Walls Gallery, San Francisco.
Robert Hudson. 25 March–11 April 1970.

1971

Allan Frumkin Gallery, New York. *Robert
Hudson: New Sculpture.* 6 April–1 May 1971.

University Art Museum, University of
California, Berkeley. *The Star Show.*
4–29 August 1971.

1972

Allan Frumkin Gallery, Chicago.
Robert Hudson: Recent Sculpture.
22 September–26 October 1972.

1973

San Francisco Museum of Art. *Robert
Hudson/Richard Shaw: Work in Porcelain.*
11 May–1 July 1973. Catalog published,
text by Suzanne Foley.

Hansen Fuller Gallery, San Francisco.
Robert Hudson: Paintings.
27 November–24 December 1973.

1974

E.G. Gallery, Kansas City, Missouri. *Robert
Hudson/Richard Shaw: Work in Porcelain.*
4 April–11 May 1974.

1975

Hansen Fuller Gallery, San Francisco.
Robert Hudson: Paintings and Sculptures.
15 April–10 May 1975.

1976

Allan Frumkin Gallery, Chicago. *Robert
Hudson.* 20 February–25 March 1976.

Allan Frumkin Gallery, New York. *Robert
Hudson.* 18 September–22 October 1976.
Catalog published, text by Jan Butterfield.

1977

Hansen Fuller Gallery, San Francisco.
Robert Hudson. 22 March–23 April 1977.

Portland Center for the Visual Arts,
Oregon. *Robert Hudson.* 2 May–3 June 1977.

Institute of Contemporary Art, Boston.
*Two California Artists: Robert Hudson and Roy
De Forest.* 9 November–11 December 1977.

Moore College of Art Gallery, Philadelphia.
Robert Hudson. 9 December 1977–27 January
1978. Catalog published, foreword by Dianne
Perry Vanderlip, text by Peter Schjeldahl.

1978

Allan Frumkin Gallery, New York.
Robert Hudson: New Paintings and Drawings.
30 September–2 November 1978.

1979

Hansen Fuller Gallery, San Francisco.
Robert Hudson. 1–26 May 1979.

South Campus Art Gallery, Miami-Dade
Community College, Florida.
*Robert Hudson: Paintings, Constructions, and
Drawings.* 29 October–15 November 1979.

1981

Allan Frumkin Gallery New York.
Robert Hudson. 28 February–26 March 1981.

1982

Fuller Goldeen Gallery, San Francisco.
Robert Hudson. 1–31 December 1982.
Brochure published.

1983

Richard L. Nelson Gallery, University of
California, Davis. *Robert Hudson: Sculpture
and Drawings.* 22 February–25 March 1983.
Catalog published, texts by L. Price
Amerson, Jr., and Rene di Rosa.

Morgan Gallery, Shawnee Mission, Missouri.
The Bob Hudson Show. 29 April–23 May 1983.

1984

Allan Frumkin Gallery, New York. *Robert
Hudson: New Polychrome Sculpture.*
31 March–3 May 1984. Catalog published,
text by David S. Rubin.

Richard Eugene Fuller Art Gallery, Beaver
College, Glenside, Pennsylvania. *Robert
Hudson: Paintings and Works on Paper.*
4–26 April 1984.

GROUP EXHIBITIONS

1958

Larsen Gallery, Yakima Valley College,
Yakima, Washington. *Washington Art
Association Exhibit.* 2–28 November 1958.

1959

Richmond Art Center, California.
*Eighth Annual Watercolor/Graphic/Ceramic
Sculpture Exhibition.* 18 June–26 July 1959.

1960

San Francisco Museum of Art.
*The Twenty-third Annual Drawing, Print, and
Watercolor Exhibition of the San Francisco Art
Association.* 15 January–14 February 1960.
Catalog published, foreword by
George D. Culler.

San Francisco Museum of Art. *San Francisco
Art Association Seventy-ninth Annual: Painting
and Sculpture.* 24 March–24 April 1960.

Richmond Art Center, California.
Tenth Annual Oil and Sculpture Exhibition.
28 October–6 December 1960.

Oakland Art Museum. *Northern California
Sculptors' Annual.* 7–26 December 1960.
Catalog published, foreword by Paul Mills.

1961

Art Center in La Jolla, California.
*Art Center Annual California
Painting and Sculpture Exhibition.*
29 October–10 December 1961.
Catalog published, foreword by
Thomas M. Messer.

San Francisco Museum of Art. *Art of San
Francisco: Ninetieth Anniversary Exhibition
of the San Francisco Art Institute.*
29 November 1961–7 January 1962.

1962

Bolles Gallery, San Francisco.
Two Obscurities...And a Sculptor.
8 January–3 February 1962.

San Francisco Museum of Art. *The Arts
of San Francisco: Painting and Sculpture.*
2 June–2 September 1962.

Stanford University Art Gallery and
Museum, California. *Some Points of View '62:
San Francisco Bay Area Painting and Sculpture.*
30 October–20 November 1962. Catalog
published, foreword by George D. Culler.

1963

San Francisco Museum of Art. *The 82nd
Annual Exhibition of the San Francisco Art
Institute.* 21 March–21 April 1963. Catalog
published.

Diego Rivera Gallery, San Francisco Art
Institute. *Some New Art in the Bay Area.*
8–24 May 1963. Brochure published,
text by Fred Martin.

Roof Garden, Kaiser Center Art Gallery, Oakland (co-sponsored by the Oakland Art Museum Guild, *Artforum* magazine, and the Oakland Art Museum). *Contemporary California Sculpture.* 4 August–15 September 1963.

Art Center in La Jolla, California. *Fourth Art Center Annual of California Painting and Sculpture.* 17 November–15 December 1963. Catalog published.

1964

San Francisco Museum of Art. *The Eighty-third Annual Exhibition of the San Francisco Art Institute.* 17 April–17 May 1964. Catalog published, introduction by George D. Culler.

Allan Frumkin Gallery, Chicago. *Gallery Artists.* June–August 1964.

San Francisco Museum of Art. *The Arts of San Francisco, Part II.* 7 August–6 September 1964.

Diego Rivera Gallery, San Francisco Art Institute. *Polychrome Sculpture.* 11 August–4 September 1964.

Cabrillo Music Festival, Aptos, California. *Art Exhibition.* 21–23, 28–30 August 1964.

Stanford University Art Gallery and Museum, California. *Current Painting and Sculpture of the Bay Area.* 8 October–29 November 1964. Catalog published, introduction by Lorenz Eitner.

Lanyon Gallery, Palo Alto, California. *Gallery Artists.* 11 November–31 December 1964.

Whitney Museum of American Art, New York. *Annual Exhibition 1964: Contemporary American Sculpture.* 9 December 1964–31 January 1965. Catalog published.

1965

California Palace of the Legion of Honor, San Francisco. *The Drawing Society–Regional Exhibition.* 27 February–11 April 1965. Catalog published, foreword by E. Gunther Troche.

College Art Gallery, San Jose State College, California. *The Inauguration Exhibition.* 26 April–14 May 1965. Catalog published.

Whitney Museum of American Art, New York. *Young America 1965: Thirty American Artists under Thirty-Five.* 23 June–29 August 1965. Catalog published, foreword by Lloyd Goodrich.

American Express Pavilion, New York World's Fair. *Young American Sculpture– East to West.* Catalog published, text by Brian O'Doherty.

1966

The Arts Council, YMHA, Philadelphia. *How the West Was Done.* 9–31 March 1966. Brochure published.

Richmond Art Center, California. *2D/3D.* 11 March–17 April 1966. Catalog published, introduction by H.J. Weeks.

Berkeley Gallery, San Francisco. *The Slant Step Show.* 9–17 September 1966.

Whitney Museum of American Art, New York. *Annual Exhibition 1966: Contemporary Sculpture and Prints.* 16 December 1966–5 February 1967. Catalog published.

1967

University Art Museum, University of California, Berkeley. *Funk.* 18 April–29 May 1967. Catalog published, text by Peter Selz.

Los Angeles County Museum of Art. *American Sculpture of the Sixties.* 28 April–25 June 1967 (traveled to Philadelphia Museum of Art, 15 September–29 October 1967). Catalog published, introduction by Maurice Tuchman, texts by Lawrence Alloway, Dore Ashton, Clement Greenberg, Barbara Rose, and others.

The Art Institute of Chicago. *Sculpture: A Generation of Innovation.* 23 June–27 August 1967. Catalog published.

University Art Museum, University of California, Berkeley. *Faculty Show.* 21 November–31 December 1967.

1968

Portland Art Museum, Oregon. *The West Coast Now: Current Work from the Western Seaboard.* 9 February–6 March 1968 (traveled to Seattle Art Museum, 21 March–21 April 1968; M.H. de Young Memorial Museum, San Francisco, 15 May–15 June 1968; Los Angeles Municipal Art Gallery, 22 August–22 September 1968). Catalog published, foreword by Rachael Griffin.

San Francisco Museum of Art. *On Looking Back: Bay Area 1945–1960.* 10 August–8 September 1968.

Whitney Museum of American Art, New York. *1968 Annual Exhibition: Contemporary American Sculpture.* 17 December 1968–9 February 1969. Catalog published.

1969

Krannert Art Museum, University of Illinois, Urbana-Champaign. *Contemporary American Painting and Sculpture 1969.* 2 March–6 April 1969. Catalog published, introduction by James R. Shipley and Allen S. Weller.

Berkeley Gallery, San Francisco. *Repair Show.* 13 March–4 April 1969.

San Francisco Museum of Art. *Just Yesterday.* 25 April–1 June 1969.

Walker Art Center and Dayton's Department Store, Minneapolis. *14 Sculptors: The Industrial Edge.* 29 May–21 June 1969. Catalog published, texts by Barbara Rose, Christopher French, and Martin Friedman.

Institute of Contemporary Art, University of Pennsylvania, Philadelphia. *The Spirit of the Comics.* 1 October–9 November 1969. Catalog published, text by Joan C. Siegfried.

1970

Indianapolis Museum of Art (organized with the Contemporary Art Society). *Painting and Sculpture Today.* 21 April–1 June 1970. Catalog published, introduction by Richard Warrum.

Joslyn Art Museum, Omaha. *Looking West 1970.* 18 October–29 November 1970. Catalog published, introduction by LeRoy Butler.

University Art Museum, University of California, Berkeley. *University of California, Berkeley, Art Faculty Show.* 7 November 1970–9 January 1971. Brochure published.

University Art Museum, University of California, Berkeley. *Impossible Dream* (performance with William T. Wiley and others). 8 November 1970.

Whitney Museum of American Art, New York. *1970 Annual Exhibition: Contemporary American Sculpture.* 12 December 1970–7 February 1971. Catalog published, foreword by John I. H. Baur.

1971

La Jolla Museum of Art, California. *Continuing Surrealism.* 15 January–21 March 1971. Catalog published, introduction by Lawrence Urrutia.

M.H. de Young Memorial Museum, San Francisco (organized by the San Francisco Art Institute). *San Francisco Art Institute Centennial Exhibition.* 15 January–28 February 1971. Catalog published, introduction by Philip Linhares.

The Art Galleries, University of California, Santa Barbara. *Six Californians.* 6 April–16 May 1971.

Allan Frumkin Gallery, New York. *Gallery and Invitational Group Exhibition.* 6 September–2 October 1971.

Denver Art Museum. *The 73rd Western Annual.* 3 October–21 November 1971. Catalog published.

Art Gallery, Saint Mary's College, Moraga, California. *The Good Drawing Show.* 30 October–26 November 1971. Catalog published.

1972

David Stuart Gallery, Los Angeles.
The Cup Show. 3–28 October 1972.

1973

Hoffman Gallery, Oregon School of Arts
and Crafts, Portland. *Artclay.*
2 October–November 1973.

Rental Gallery, The Baltimore Museum
of Art. *Art from the San Francisco Bay Area.*
14 October–31 November 1973.

1974

Emanuel Walter Gallery, San Francisco Art
Institute. *Ceramic Sculpture.* 5–31 March 1974.
Brochure published, text by Philip Linhares.

Krannert Art Museum, University
of Illinois, Urbana-Champaign. *Contemporary
American Painting and Sculpture.*
10 March–21 April 1974. Catalog
published, introduction by James R. Shipley
and Allen S. Weller.

Margo Leavin Gallery, Los Angeles. *Drawings.*
11 April–11 May 1974.

Whitney Museum of American Art,
Downtown Branch, New York. *Clay.*
23 May–4 July 1974. Catalog published,
text by Richard Marshall.

Fine Arts Gallery, University of Nevada, Las
Vegas. *The Nicholas Wilder Collection: Portrait
of an Art Dealer.* 2–27 September 1974.

1975

Newport Harbor Art Museum, Newport
Beach, California. *A Drawing Show.*
26 January–9 March 1975 (traveled to
Walnut Creek Civic Arts Gallery, California,
19 March–3 May 1975). Catalog published,
text by Betty Turnbull.

The Corcoran Gallery of Art, Washington,
D.C. *34th Biennial of Contemporary American
Painting.* 22 February–6 April 1975. Catalog
published, introduction by Roy Slade.

Fendrick Gallery, Washington, D.C. *Clay U.S.A.*
11 March–12 April 1975. Catalog published,
introduction by Daniel Fendrick.

Hayward Gallery, London (organized by the
Arts Council of Great Britain). *The Condition
of Sculpture.* 29 May–13 July 1975. Catalog
published, preface by Robin Campbell and
Joanna Drew, introduction by William Tucker.

National Collection of Fine Arts,
Smithsonian Institution, Washington, D.C.
Sculpture: American Directions 1945–1975.
3 October–30 November 1975.
Catalog published.

Helen Euphrat Gallery, De Anza College,
Cupertino, California. *A Survey of Sculptural
Directions in the Bay Area.* 8–30 October 1975.
Catalog published, introduction
by Erin Goodwin.

Hansen Fuller Gallery, San Francisco. *Hansen
Fuller Gallery Pays Tribute to the San Francisco
Art Institute, Part II.* 11–29 November 1975.

1976

San Francisco Museum of Modern Art,
*Painting and Sculpture in California:
The Modern Era.*
3 September–21 November 1976
(traveled to National Collection of Fine
Arts, Smithsonian Institution, Washington,
D.C., 20 May–11 September 1977). Catalog
published, texts by Henry T. Hopkins,
Katherine Church Holland, and others.

Dalhousie Art Gallery, Halifax,
Nova Scotia. *3 From California.*
15 November–15 December 1976.
Catalog published.

Darwin Gallery, Sonoma State College,
Rohnert Park, California. *Overview.*
November–December 1976.

1977

William Hayes Ackland Memorial Art
Center, The University of North Carolina,
Chapel Hill. *Contemporary Ceramic Sculpture.*
6 February–6 March 1977. Catalog published,
text by Louise Hobbs.

Huntsville Museum of Art, Alabama.
California Bay Area Art: Update 1970–1977.
6 May–31 July 1977.

Archer M. Huntington Gallery, The
University of Texas, Austin. *New in the
Seventies.* 21 August–25 September 1977.
Catalog published, foreword by Donald B.
Goodall, text by Fred Seabolt.

Olin Art Gallery, Whitman College, Walla
Walla, Washington. *III California Artists.*
1–30 September 1977.

Madison Art Center, Wisconsin. *Recent
Works on Paper by American Artists.*
4 December 1977–15 January 1978. Catalog
published, introduction by Victor Kord,
text by Joseph Wilfer.

1978

San Francisco Museum of Modern Art.
Aesthetics of Graffiti. 28 April–2 July 1978.
Catalog published, texts by Rolando
Castellón and Howard J. Pearlstein.

John Michael Kohler Arts Center,
Sheboygan, Wisconsin. *Clay from Molds:
Multiples, Altered Castings, Combinations.*
19 June–6 August 1978. Catalog published.

1979

Sara Spurgeon Gallery, Central
Washington University, Ellensburg. *Second
Annual Invitational Drawing Exhibition.*
5 February–2 March 1979.

Denver Art Museum (organized by the
Western States Arts Foundation with
assistance from the Denver Art Museum
and the National Collection of Fine Arts).
The First Western States Biennial Exhibition.
7 March–15 April 1979 (traveled to National

Collection of Fine Arts, Washington, D.C.,
8 June–3 September 1979;
San Francisco Museum of Modern Art,
26 October–9 December 1979; Seattle Art
Museum, 29 May–13 July 1980). Catalog
published, preface by Richard L. Harcourt
and Thomas N. Maytham, introduction
by Joshua C. Taylor, text by Robert A. Ewing.

Odyssia Gallery, New York. *The Pastel in
America.* 8 May–16 June 1979 (traveled to
Grand Rapids Art Museum, Michigan,
6 August–16 September 1979). Catalog
published, introduction by Irving Petlin.

Hirshhorn Museum and Sculpture Garden,
Smithsonian Institution, Washington, D.C.
Directions. 14 June–3 September 1979.
Catalog published, foreword by Abraham
Lerner, introduction by Howard N. Fox.

Frumkin & Struve Gallery, Chicago. *Large
Drawings.* 1 November–8 December 1979.

1980

San Diego Museum of Art. *Sculpture
in California 1975–80.* 18 May–6 July 1980.
Catalog published, foreword by Steven L.
Brezzo, text by Richard Armstrong.

The Palo Alto Cultural Center, California.
Painted Sculpture. 31 August–26 October 1980.

Norman Mackenzie Art Gallery, University
of Regina, Saskatchewan. *The Continental Clay
Connection.* 12 September–19 October 1980.
Catalog published.

1981

The Aldrich Museum of Contemporary Art,
Ridgefield, Connecticut. *New Dimensions in
Drawing 1950–1980.* 2 May–6 September 1981.
Catalog published, introduction by
Richard E. Anderson.

Fuller Goldeen Gallery, San Francisco.
Polychrome. 2 December 1981–2 January 1982.

1982

Mills College Art Gallery, Oakland. *Visiting
Artists Group Show.* 26 January–7 March 1982.

Museum of Fine Arts, Boston. *A Private
Vision: Contemporary Art from the Graham
Gund Collection.* 9 February–4 April 1982.
Catalog published, foreword by Jan Fontein,
preface by Graham Gund, texts by Carl
Belz, Kathy Halbreich, Kenworth Moffett,
Elisabeth Sussman, and Diane W. Upright.

Palm Springs Desert Museum, California.
*The West as Art: Changing Perceptions
of Western Art in California Collections.*
24 February–30 May 1982. Catalog
published, foreword by Alexander Stoia,
text by Patricia Jean Trenton.

Allan Frumkin Gallery, New York. *Summer
Gallery Group Show.* 8 June–14 August 1982.

Alberta College of Art Gallery, Calgary.
First Annual Wild West Show.
24 June–31 July 1982. Catalog published,
text by Val Greenfield.

The Oakland Museum. *100 Years of California
Sculpture.* 7 August–17 October 1982. Catalog
published, preface by Christina Orr-Cahall,
texts by Paul Tomidy, Harvey L. Jones,
Terry St. John, and Christopher Knight.

De Saisset Museum, University of Santa
Clara, California. *Northern California Art of
the Sixties.* 12 October–12 December 1982.
Catalog published, introduction by
Georgianna M. Lagoria, texts by Fred Martin
and Georgianna M. Lagoria.

1983

Fuller Goldeen Gallery, San Francisco.
Selections I. 4 May–4 June 1983.

Morgan Gallery, Kansas City, Missouri.
Thanking the Muse.
18 September–6 October 1983.

Nassau County Museum of Fine Art, Roslyn
Harbor, New York. *Sculpture: The Tradition
in Steel.* 9 October 1983–22 January 1984.
Catalog published, text by Janice Parente
and Phyllis Stigliano.

Foster Gallery, University of Wisconsin, Eau
Claire. *The New Morgan Gallery Presents.*
18 October–11 November 1983.

1984

Richard L. Nelson Gallery, University of
California, Davis. *Painters at UC Davis, Part II:
1970s–1980s.* 26 February–30 March 1984.
Catalog published, preface by L. Price
Amerson, Jr.

Palm Springs Desert Museum, California.
Return of the Narrative. 17 March–3 June 1984.
Catalog published, foreword by
Morton Golden, text by Katherine Plake
Hough and Roberta Arnold Cove.

DeCordova Museum, Lincoln,
Massachusetts. *A Passionate Vision:
Contemporary Ceramics from the Daniel
Jacobs Collection.* 1 April–27 May 1984.
Catalog published, introduction by Maria
Friedrich, texts by Michael McTwigan
and Daniel Jacobs.

Fisher Gallery, University of Southern
California, Los Angeles (organized by the
California/International Arts Foundation as
part of the 1984 Olympic Arts Festival).
California Sculpture Show. 2 June–12 August
1984 (traveled to C.A.P.C. Musée d'Art
Contemporain de Bordeaux, France,
October 1984; Stadtiche Kuntshalle,
Mannheim, West Germany, February 1985;
Yorkshire Sculpture Park, West Bretton,
England, May 1985; Sonja Henies og Niels
Onstads Stiftelser, Hovikodden, Norway,
September 1985). Catalog published,
introduction by Robert J. Fitzpatrick,
foreword by Henry T. Hopkins, texts
by Jan Butterfield and Melinda Wortz.

A.P. Giannini Gallery, Bank of America
World Headquarters, San Francisco.
*Highlights: Selections from the BankAmerica
Corporation Art Collection.*
11 October–27 November 1984.
Brochure published.

Fuller Goldeen Gallery, San Francisco.
Stars: A Theme Exhibition.
4 December 1984–5 January 1985.

1985

Museum of Art, Rhode Island School of
Design, Providence. *Fortissimo! Thirty Years
from the Richard Brown Baker Collection of
Contemporary Art.* 1 March–28 April 1985
(will travel to San Diego Museum of Art,
29 July–25 August 1985; Portland Museum of
Art, Oregon, 1 October–10 November 1985).
Catalog published, text by Richard
Brown Baker.

Dayton Art Institute, Ohio. *Clay.*
19 March–16 June 1985. Catalog published,
introduction by Pam Houk.

Des Moines Art Center. *Iowa Collects.*
2 May–30 June 1985. Catalog published, text
by James T. Demetrion.

Bibliography

compiled by Eugenie Candau

BOOKS

Anderson, Wayne. *American Sculpture in Process: 1930–1970.* Boston: New York Graphic Society, 1975, p. 161-162, 163, ill.

Beal, Graham W. J., and John Perreault. *Wiley Territory.* Minneapolis: Walker Art Center, 1979, p. 8, 10. Ex. cat.

Clark, Garth. *A Century of Ceramics in the United States, 1878–1978.* New York: E.P. Dutton in association with the Everson Museum of Art, 1979, p. xxiv, 159, 298-299, 307, 327, ill. p. 232, 233.

50 West Coast Artists. San Francisco: Chronicle Books, 1981, p. 22, 46-47, 64, ill.

Harrington, LaMar. *Ceramics in the Pacific Northwest.* Seattle: University of Washington Press for the Henry Art Gallery, 1979, p. 113.

Kuspit, Donald. *The Critic Is Artist: The Intentionality of Art.* Ann Arbor: UMI Research Press, 1984, p. 287. Reprint of "Regionalism Reconsidered," *Art in America,* July–August 1976.

Orr-Cahall, Christina, ed. *The Art of California: Selected Works from the Collection of The Oakland Museum.* Oakland: Oakland Museum, 1984, p. 34, 150, 192, ill.

Plagens, Peter. *Sunshine Muse: Contemporary Art on the West Coast.* New York: Praeger, 1974, p. 87, 88, 89, 99, ill. p. 68.

San Francisco Museum of Modern Art: The Painting and Sculpture Collection. New York: Hudson Hills Press, 1985, p. 24, 224, 228, 232-233, 258, 317-318, ill.

ARTICLES

An R following an entry indicates a review. An asterisk preceding an item indicates that it was not available for examination by the compiler.

1960

Cross, Miriam Dungan. "You Can't Be Too Busy to See Remarkable Museum Exhibits." *Oakland Tribune,* 18 December 1960, p. C3. R.

1962

Coplans, John. "Angel-Hipsterism, Beat and Zen versus New Materials." *Artforum,* September 1962, p. 39, ill. p. 40. R.

Frankenstein, Alfred. "'Obscurities' in a Gallery." *This World, San Francisco Sunday Chronicle,* 14 January 1962, p. 27. R.

*Fried, Alexander. "A Fine Young Talent Wins Recognition on the Rebound." *San Francisco Examiner,* January 1962, ill. R.

M[artin], F[red]. "Sugai Paintings and Hudson Drawings." *Artforum,* August 1962, p. 38. R.

"Notes on Bay Area Art and Artists." *Oakland Tribune,* 7 January 1962, p. EL-5. R.

1963

Coplans, John. "Sculpture in California." *Artforum,* August 1963, p. 5, ill. p. 31.

Leider, Philip. "California after the Figure." *Art in America,* October 1963, p. 77, ill. p. 79.

L[eider], P[hilip]. "Some New Art in the Bay Area" in "Reviews." *Artforum,* July 1963, p. 7. R.

M[onte], J[ames]. "82nd Annual Exhibition of the San Francisco Art Institute." *Artforum,* May 1963, p. 11, ill. R.

———. "Group Show, New Mission Gallery" in "Reviews." *Artforum,* June 1963, p. 45. R.

P[olley], E[lizabeth] M. "Young Artists" in "Reviews." *Artforum,* March 1963, p. 12, ill. p. 13. R.

1964

Coplans, John. "Circle of Styles on the West Coast." *Art in America,* June 1964, p. 30, ill. p. 28.

Frankenstein, Alfred. "A Break with Art Tradition." *This World, San Francisco Sunday Chronicle,* 26 April 1964, p. 21-22. R.

Fried, Alexander. "Sluggish Tide of New S.F. Acquisitions." *Show Time, San Francisco Examiner,* 15 March 1964, p. 18, ill. R.

Fuller, Mary. "San Francisco Sculptors." *Art in America,* June 1964, p. 59.

Kind, Joshua. "Chicago." *Art News,* September 1964, p. 52. R.

Kline, D.H. "The 'Fly-By' Knight." *Study Magazine* (San Jose City College), September 1964, p. 11-13. Ed. note and poem.

Kozloff, Max. "West Coast Art: Vital Pathology." *The Nation,* 24 August 1964, p. 76, 79. R.

Leider, Philip. "Three San Francisco Sculptors." *Artforum,* September 1964, cover and p. 36, 38-39, ill.

M[agloff], J[oanna] C. "Group Show, Lanyon Gallery" in "San Francisco." *Artforum,* January 1964, p. 11. R.

Magloff, Joanna. "San Francisco." *Art News,* January 1964, p. 51. R.

M[onte], J[ames]. "Current Painting and Sculpture of the Bay Area" in "San Francisco." *Artforum,* December 1964, p. 47. R.

Monte, James. "Polychrome Sculpture." *Artforum,* November 1964, p. 41, 42. R.

———. "Sculpture Steals the Show in the 83rd Annual." *Artforum,* May 1964, p. 24, ill. p. 22. R.

R[euschel], J[ohn]. "Fourth Annual of California Painting and Sculpture" in "Los Angeles." *Artforum,* January 1964, p. 43. R.

"Sculpture: Era of the Object." *Time,* 11 December 1964, p. 84, ill. p. 85. R.

Ventura, Anita. "San Francisco." *Arts Magazine,* October 1964, p. 24. R.

1965

Ashton, Dore. "Life and Movement without Recession: New York Commentary." *Studio International,* December 1965, p. 252. R.

Boone, Charles. "A Legion Exhibit Unveils Famous 'September Morn.'" *Show Time, San Francisco Examiner,* 29 August 1965, p. 18, ill. R.

Bourdon, David. "Art: Follow the Dotted Lines." *Village Voice,* 21 October 1965, p. 11. R.

Constable, Rosalind. "Is It Painting or Is It Sculpture?" *Life International,* 20 December 1965, p. 132, ill.

Coplans, John. "West Coast Notes." *Art International,* February 1965, p. 46, ill. p. 47. R.

Davis, Douglas M. "Taking the Art World's Pulse: Op, Near-Op, Off-Op—and Eros." *The National Observer,* 30 August 1965, p. 18. R.

Frankenstein, Alfred. "Two Modern Sculptors." *San Francisco Chronicle,* 2 September 1965, p. 41, ill. R.

Kozloff, Max. "The Further Adventures of American Sculpture." *Arts Magazine,* February 1965, p. 31, ill.

Monte, James. "San Francisco." *Artforum,* November 1965, p. 45, 47, ill. R.

Pincus-Witten, Robert. [Robert Hudson] in "New York." *Artforum,* December 1965, p. 53. R.

R[obins], C[orinne ?]. "In the Galleries: Robert Hudson." *Arts,* December 1965, p. 55, ill. p. 54. R.

Rosenthal, Nan. "New York: Gallery Notes." *Art in America,* April 1965, p. 122, ill. R.

"Sculptor Robert Hudson Receives Nealie Sullivan Award of $1000." *San Francisco Art Institute News,* July 1965, p. [1].

1966

Adrian, Dennis. "Group Sculpture Show, World House" in "New York." *Artforum,* January 1966, p. 56. R.

1967

Adrian, Dennis. "Sculpture and Print Annual, Whitney Museum" in "New York." *Artforum,* March 1967, p. 56, ill. p. 54. R.

*Ashton, Dore. "Jeunes talents de la sculpture Américaine." *Aujourd 'hui,* January 1967, p. 160.

Danieli, Fidel A. "American Sculpture of the Sixties at the Los Angeles County Museum." *Studio International,* June 1967, p. 321, ill. R.

———. "Robert Hudson: Space and Camouflage." *Artforum,* November 1967, p. 32-35, ill.

Halstead, Whitney. "Chicago." *Artforum,* October 1967, p. 65. R.

Monte James, "'Making It' with Funk." *Artforum,* June 1967, p. 57, ill. p. 56. R.

Seldis, Henry J. "Sculpture of the Sixties." *West, Los Angeles Times*, 4 June 1967, p. 39, ill. R.

————. "U.S. Sculpture Exhibit Looks beyond the 60s." *Calendar, Los Angeles Times*, 7 May 1967, p. 38. R.

"The Third Dimension." *Newsweek*, 8 May 1967, p. 92, ill. p. 93, 94. R.

Tuten, Frederic. "American Sculpture of the Sixties." *Arts Magazine*, May 1967, ill. p. 42, 43. R.

Wilson, William. "Six Robert Hudson Sculptures Displayed." *Los Angeles Times*, 8 December 1967, IV, p. 9. R.

1968

Livingston, Jane. "Los Angeles." *Artforum*, February 1968, p. 61, ill. R.

1970

Albright, Thomas. "Fabulous Art Sale at U.C." *San Francisco Chronicle*, 31 December 1970, p. 27.

Friedman, Martin. "14 Sculptors: The Industrial Edge." *Art International*, February 1970, p. 38, 40, 50, ill.

McCann, Cecile N. "Hudson Images of Tension." *Artweek*, 4 April 1970, p. 1, ill. R.

————. "U.C. Berkeley Faculty Show." *Artweek*, 26 December 1970, p. 1. R.

Richardson, Brenda. "Bay Area Galleries." *Arts Magazine*, Summer 1970, p. 51, ill.

————. "Bay Area Survey: The Myth of Neo-Dada." *Arts Magazine*, Summer 1970, p. 48.

Tarshis, Jerome. "San Francisco." *Artforum*, September 1970, p. 90, ill. R.

1971

Atirnomis. "Robert Hudson" in "New York Galleries." *Arts Magazine*, May 1971, p. 64. R.

Fitz Gibbon, John. "Sacramento!" *Art in America*, November 1971, p. 79, 80, 81.

H[enry], G[errit]. "Robert Hudson" in "Reviews and Previews." *Art News*, Summer 1971, p. 14. R.

"Hudson's Stars." *Artweek*, 7 August 1971, p. 5.

Linville, Kasha. "Robert Hudson, Frumkin Gallery." *Artforum*, June 1971, p. 86, ill. R.

M[cCann], C[ecile] N. "Robert Hudson." *Artweek*, 21 August 1971, p. 8, ill. R.

Muldavin, Albie, and John Noel Chandler. "Correspondences." *Artscanada*, June-July 1971, p. 44, 45, 47, 48, 52, 54, 55, 60, 61, ill.

Richardson, Brenda. "San Francisco." *Arts Magazine*, September-October 1971, p. 54, ill. R.

Stiles, Knute. "A Centennial in San Francisco: Three Museums Celebrate 100 Years of the San Francisco Art Institute." *Artforum*, April 1971, p. 72, ill. R.

Zack, David. "West Coast: Bay Area Gallery Innovations." *Art and Artists*, January 1971, p. 60, ill. p. 61.

1973

Frankenstein, Alfred. "Revolution in Ceramics." *San Francisco Chronicle*, 17 May 1973, p. 50, ill. R.

Fried, Alexander. "Another Side to Two Artists." *San Francisco Examiner*, 28 November 1973, p. 42, ill. R.

McCann, Cecile N. "Hudson and Shaw." *Artweek*, 9 June 1973, p. 1, 3, ill. R.

————. "Robert Hudson Paintings." *Artweek*, 15 December 1973, p. 1, 16, ill. R.

McChesney, Mary Fuller. "Porcelain by Richard Shaw and Robert Hudson." *Craft Horizons*, October 1973, p. 34-37, ill. R.

Meisel, Alan. "San Francisco." *Craft Horizons*, August 1973, p. 26, ill. R.

"Porcelain by Robert Hudson and Richard Shaw." *Ceramics Monthly*, September 1973, p. 60, ill.

Shere, Charles. "Museum of Art Shows Display Style, Wit." *Oakland Tribune*, 3 June 1973, p. 28-EN, ill. R.

Tarshis, Jerome. "Letter from San Francisco." *Studio International*, November 1973, p. 193.

————. "A Wyeth Show and Some Others." *Art News*, September 1973, p. 62. R.

1974

McCann, Cecile N. "Ceramic Sculpture." *Artweek*, 16 March 1974, p. 16, R.

Shere, Charles. "Richmond Presents Encore." *Oakland Tribune*, 10 February 1974, p. 30. R.

Tarshis, Jerome. "Struggling with Success." *Art News*, March 1974, p. 78. R.

1975

Albright, Thomas. "Mythmakers." *Art Gallery*, February 1975, p. 16, 45.

"Bob Hudson: Like Reading a Road Map." [Interview with] John Marlowe. *Currant*, April-May 1975, p. 33. ill.

Chapman, Hilary. "The Condition of Sculpture 1975." *Arts Magazine*, November 1975, p. 69, ill.

Coffelt, Beth. "End of the Game." *California Living, San Francisco Sunday Examiner and Chronicle*, 18 May 1975, p. 7, 8, 9, ill.

Frankenstein, Alfred. "A Serene Work of Pure Space." *San Francisco Chronicle*, 20 November 1975, p. 48, ill. R.

————. "Two Artistic Approaches." *San Francisco Chronicle*, 29 April 1975, p. 40, ill. R.

Koslow, Francine. "Robert Hudson, New Work." *Artweek*, 3 May 1975, p. 7, ill. R.

Shere, Charles. "Absorbing Walnut Creek Show." *Oakland Tribune*, 30 March 1975, p. 30-E, ill. R.

Wilson, William. "Double-Edged Message in 'A Drawing Show.'" *Calendar, Los Angeles Times*, 16 February 1975, p. 62. R.

1976

Bourdon, David. "Decorative Is Not a Dirty Word." *Village Voice*, 11 October 1976, p. 96, ill. R.

Brown, Sylvia. "Robert Hudson at Hansen-Fuller." *Art in America*, January-February 1976, p. 105-106, ill. R.

Davis, Douglas. "The Two Faces of California." *Newsweek*, 6 September 1976, p. 52, ill. R.

Ellenzweig, Allen. "Robert Hudson." *Arts Magazine*, December 1976, p. 31, ill. R.

Frank, Peter. "Robert Hudson" in "New York Reviews." *Art News*, November 1976, p. 149, ill. p. 150. R.

Kramer, Hilton. "Art." *New York Times*, 1 October 1976, p. C 14. R.

Kuspit, Donald B. "Regionalism Reconsidered." *Art in America*, July-August 1976, p. 67. Reprinted in Donald Kuspit, *The Critic Is Artist*, Ann Arbor: UMI Research Press, 1984.

Muchnic, Suzanne. "A Capsule History of Modern Sculpture." *Artweek*, 6 November 1976, p. 7. R.

"Richland to Bay Area: A Shared Experience." *Allan Frumkin Gallery Newsletter*, Fall 1976, p. 1-2.

Schapiro, Lindsay Stamm. "New York/ Sculpture." *Craft Horizons*, December 1976, p. 53. R. Weeks, H.J.

"Bay Area Sculpture Survey." *Artweek*, 6 March 1976, p. 9. R.

1977

Albright, Thomas. "Hudson: In the Shadow of Wiley." *San Francisco Chronicle*, 29 March 1977, p. 40. R.

————. "Meditations on 11 Purring Cats." *Art News*, September 1977, p. 122. R.

"Bay Area Artist Receives Guggenheim." *Artweek*, 14 May 1977, p. 4.

Bloomfield, Arthur. "Artist Takes Imagination on a Joy Ride." *San Francisco Examiner*, 25 March 1977, p. 34, ill. R.

Brown, Sylvia. "Bay Area Sculpture." *Visual Dialog*, June-August 1977, p. 2, 4, 5, 6, ill.

Dickson, Joanne A. "Remembering the Lanyon Gallery." *Visual Dialog*, Fall 1977, p. 21, 23, 24, ill.

Dills, Keith. "Robert Hudson's New Work." *Artweek*, 16 April 1977, p. 1, 6, ill. R.

*Donohoe, Victoria. "Hudson Baffles and Entertains with His Kitchen-Sink Esthetic." *Philadelphia Inquirer*, 18 December 1977, ill. R.

*Forman, Nessa. "Something You Can Look at Without Getting Bored." *Sunday Bulletin* (Philadelphia), 18 December 1977, ill. R.

"Gallery Rundown: Summer Summary." *Allan Frumkin Gallery Newsletter,* Fall 1977, p. 3, ill.

1978

Bradley, Laurel. "Robert Hudson." *Arts Magazine,* December 1978, p. 24, ill. p. 25, R.

Larson, Kay. "Robert Hudson." *Art News,* December 1978, p. 141, 143, ill. R.

Witt, Gary, "Recent Media: A Tennessee 'Happening.'" *Art Voices/South,* March-April 1978, p. 56, ill. p. 58, R.

1979

Albright, Thomas. "At the Galleries." *San Francisco Chronicle,* 12 May 1979, p. 36. R.

Brown, Christopher. "Disparate Voices." *Artweek,* 19 May 1979, p. 1, 20, ill. R.

1981

Baro, Gene. "New York Letter." *Art International,* August-September 1981, p. 119-120. R.

1982

Burkhart, Dorothy. "The '60s Art Experience." *The Tab, San Jose Mercury News,* 17 October 1982, p. 15. R.

Platt, Susan. "Hudson's World." *Artweek,* 25 December 1982, p. 3, ill. R.

Temko, Allan. "The Happy Confusion of Robert Hudson." *San Francisco Chronicle,* 30 December 1982, p. 33, ill. R.

1983

Albright, Thomas. "Robert Hudson." *Art News,* February 1983, p. 128. R.

Boettger, Suzaan. "Robert Hudson." *Artforum,* April 1983, p. 79. R.

Stiles, Knute. "Robert Hudson at Fuller Goldeen." *Art in America,* March 1983, p. 165, ill. p. 158.

1984

Glueck, Grace. "Art." *New York Times,* 6 April 1984, p. C 28. R.

Ianco-Starrels, Josine. "Sculpture Show: USC to Europe." *Calendar, Los Angeles Times,* 27 May 1984, p. 80.

"Robert Hudson Retrospective." *Allan Frumkin Gallery Newsletter,* Summer 1984, p. 1.

FILM

Nelson, Gunvor, and Dorothy Wiley. *Five Artists: Billbobbillbillbob.* 16mm, 70 min., sound, color. 1971. Distributed by Canyon Cinema, San Francisco.